ABOUT THE AUTHOR

Boris Leonidovich Pasternak, poet, novelist
and translator of Goethe and Shakespeare, was
born in Moscow in 1890. The son of a well-
known portrait painter and a concert pianist, he
abandoned the study of music at an early age,
turning instead to philosophy and then to
writing. After the revolution, he was employed
in the library of the Ministry of Education,
and participated in the *avant-garde* investigations
of new techniques of poetry. Acclaimed in the
Twenties as the greatest Russian poet of the
post-revolutionary era, he achieved world
recognition with the publication of *Doctor
Zhivago* in 1957. He was awarded, and
declined, the Nobel Prize for Literature the
following year, and died at his home in the
"writer's village" of Peredelkino in May, 1960.

ABOUT THE TRANSLATOR

Phillip C. Flayderman, teacher, poet, editor,
and translator holds degrees from Amherst
College and Columbia University. He has taught
Russian, Latin, and German and currently
lectures on Russian literature in the School of
Continuing Education, New York University.

THE RUSSIAN LIBRARY presents masterpieces of
singular spiritual energy and freshly penetrating
style characteristic of the renaissance of
Russian literature during the nineteenth
and early twentieth centuries. The series
includes the works of both the giants and their
most noted contemporaries, all in new and
definitive translations—prime materials for
the understanding of Russia, its culture,
and its people.

The Russian Library

GENERAL EDITOR

ROBERT PAYNE

TITLES IN PRINT, FALL, 1967

SISTER MY LIFE by BORIS PASTERNAK. Translated by Phillip C. Flayderman.

THE ISLAND: A JOURNEY TO SAKHALIN by ANTON CHEKHOV. Translated by Luba and Michael Terpak.

THE TALE OF THE UNEXTINGUISHED MOON AND OTHER STORIES by BORIS PILNYAK. Translated by Beatrice Scott.

LOVE AND OTHER STORIES by YURI OLYESHA. Translated by Robert Payne.

THE COMPLETE PLAYS OF VLADIMIR MAYAKOVSKY. Translated by Guy Daniels.

IN PREPARATION

SELECTED POEMS OF ANNA AKHMATOVA. Translated by Carole W. Bartlett.

CORRESPONDENCE WITH FRIENDS by NIKOLAI GOGOL. Translated by Arthur Hudgins.

SELECTED POEMS OF OSIP MANDELSHTAM. Translated by Peter Russell.

THE APOCALYPSE OF OUR TIME by V. V. ROZANOV. Translated by Janet Romanoff.

AN ANTHOLOGY OF GEORGIAN POETRY. Translated by George Nakashidze.

AN ANTHOLOGY OF RUSSIAN POETRY. Translated by Guy Daniels.

SISTER MY LIFE

БОРИС ПАСТЕРНАК

СЕСТРА МОЯ ЖИЗНЬ

Лето 1917 года

BORIS PASTERNAK

SISTER MY LIFE

Summer, 1917

TRANSLATED BY
Phillip C. Flayderman

WASHINGTON SQUARE PRESS, INC. · NEW YORK · 1967

The frontispiece of Boris Pasternak in 1921
is from a sketch by Yuri Annenkov.

Library of Congress Catalog Number: 67-17361

Published simultaneously in the United States
and Canada by Washington Square Press, Inc.

Printed in the United States of America

TO

Marilyn, Bruce, and Stephen

INTRODUCTION

I

Toward the end of his life, when he had achieved a fame which simultaneously disturbed and pleased him — for fame was the least of his spurs — Pasternak liked to draw friends and acquaintances around him and discourse on the nature of the art he had practiced so long and so ardently and so dangerously. He especially liked to have young people around him, for he had a special fondness for youth, and he enjoyed their quick wit and gaiety. In the dining room or in the upstairs study at Peredelkino he would gather them around him, pull out books from the shelves, chant poetry, attend to the comforts of his listeners by pouring out immense quantities of kvass and vodka, and sometimes he would fall into long monologues, which were rarely about himself. Inevitably he would find himself discussing poetry as though it were some vast, little-traveled landscape beyond the horizon. There were great cities called Shakespeare, Lermontov, Pushkin, Goethe; there were small slumbering villages; there were railroad lines which vanished into the distance, and huge forbidding mountains. At such moments he was like a surveyor attempting to chart a strange land, which never ceased to fascinate him. Again and again he would return to the quest. He would change measuring rods, or simply throw them away because he found he could learn more about the country by speaking with its rare inhabitants. To the end it would remain a mysterious country, obeying its own laws and possessing its own immemorial customs. Sometimes — and this happened more frequently after the publication of *Doctor Zhivago* — he would say that poetry was a mirage, and perhaps after all there was more to be gained in the kingdom of prose.

One day, not long before his death, he was talking with some young friends at Peredelkino when someone asked him the inevitable, the longed-for question. He found himself once more traveling along familiar ground, but since the questioner was French, he felt he must reply in French, a language which he read easily and spoke with a singular disregard for grammar. "What is art?" he began, and for a while his mind hovered over the phrase of Verlaine: *"De la musique avant toute chose."* But no, art was not music — it was something far greater than music, for it was concerned with greatness itself, and he suggested that Verlaine might more justifiably have written: *"De la grandeur avant toute chose."* He went on to say that by *grandeur* he did not mean grand gestures or monuments, but something much simpler. *Grandeur* was something which could only be known by those who have spent their whole lives with a sense of pity for women and children, with charity toward all. Those who devote themselves to the human community are already on the way to greatness. Ultimately art derived from human dignity, from charity, from a sense of man's sovereign freedom. Then he said in that execrable and wonderful French which he spoke without any hesitation, as though it were a language he had invented only a few moments before: *"Il faut être libre souverainement, en roi, non par les autorités de son âge, des usages environ longs, mais de ses propres perfections acquises, franc de soi-même."*

Though he spoke with the tongues of Pentecost, the

meaning was abundantly clear. One must live in sovereign freedom like a king, never surrendering to temporal authority or traditions, however deeply rooted, but out of one's own acquired perfections in complete honesty. He was pronouncing the law, and there was some significance in the fact that the first commandment was almost beyond anyone's capacity to obey. In much the same way he went on to speak of the nature of beauty in art, saying it was *"la sublimité manifestée avec désinvolture, nonchalamment, voilà que la beauté."* We do not usually associate sublimity with nonchalance and disinterestedness, but Pasternak meant exactly what he said. He was speaking passionately and urgently, as men do when they are old. When he spoke of freedom, he did not mean the casual freedoms of everyday life, and when he spoke of traditions and authority, he did not mean only the traditions of Russia and the authoritarian state, which was continually attempting to destroy him. He spoke as though from a great distance with all the authority which was in him. He had earned the right to speak in this way, for he was the last survivor among the great poets who had given grace to the early years of the century. No doubt the commandments would change from day to day; there would be slight changes of emphasis; new ideas, new explorations would be channeled into the mainstream; but the essentials never changed. All his life he held fast to the vision of greatness expressed in those seven blinding words: *"Il faut être libre souverainement, en roi . . ."*

II

When the February Revolution broke out in Russia, the people learned for the first time in their long history what it was like to live in sovereign freedom, like kings. The monarchy, which had reigned for so long and so inadequately, crumbled to powder. The great officers of state, resplendent in their shining uniforms, accustomed to giving orders and seeing them blindly obeyed, found themselves under arrest or went into hiding. For centuries Russia had been the prisoner of her past; now the past was overthrown, and a vast exultation swept across the country.

Like everyone else in Russia, Pasternak was caught up in that storm of excitement. He had spent the war years in occupations which gave him little satisfaction: as a tutor to rich men's children, and later as the secretary of a draft board in the Urals. One of his pleasures on the draft board was to excuse large numbers of factory workers from military service, but he himself had no objection to military service and at the beginning of the war he had attempted to join up. Discharged because of an accident in his youth which left one leg shorter than the other, he continued to believe there was truth in the front lines, only lies in the rear. He had hoped for the Revolution, and when it came he could not wait to reach Moscow. An engineer attached to one of the factories was leaving posthaste for Moscow. Pasternak accompanied him. To reach the railhead they drove by sleigh through an enchanted forest still deep in the winter snow, and many years later he could still remember the sound of the hoarfrost brushing off the silver firs and the hissing of the samovar in a forest inn where they rested briefly at night. The inn resembled a brigand's lair, lost in the vastness of the forest. It was such a journey as a man might have made in the fifteenth century. Nothing had changed.

But in Moscow everything had changed: the excitement in the air was almost palpable. The Revolution had broken out in St. Petersburg, but Moscow was volubly proclaiming its newfound freedom. New political parties were being formed; the poets were issuing manifestos; the painters were announcing that henceforth paint would be applied to canvases in new, revolutionary ways. Mayakovsky, the leader of the Futurist movement, painter, poet, dramatist, master of rhetoric and vituperation, found an atmosphere exactly suited to his genius, and in those feverish days he seemed to dominate Russian poetry by the violence of his imagery and the sustained passion of his thought. He twisted language to suit his own purposes, and already he was speaking of verses as bullets fired on behalf of the Revolution. Pasternak, who had known and admired him before the war, was among the first to greet him when he arrived in Moscow a few days later. Mayakovsky was in high spirits and immediately began to read some poems from his long poem cycle *War and Peace,* an interminable diatribe against the war. It was slogan poetry of the worst kind, and Pasternak was horrified. "I made no attempt to enlarge on my impressions," Pasternak wrote later. "He read them in my eyes, and besides, he knew the extent of his influence on me." The extent of Mayakovsky's influence on Pasternak was virtually nil; they had opposing philosophies and opposing aims. Before he left, Pasternak suggested that it would be wonderful if the entire Futurist movement could be sent to the devil. To his surprise Mayakovsky half-agreed with him.

Something had gone wrong. The Revolution which had begun with such high hopes seemed to be disintegrating before men's eyes. There was no focus, no effective government. Russia was slowly drifting into anarchy, while still at war with Germany. Yet something of the wild elation of February continued into the long summer and even into the autumn of defeat.

Pasternak's meeting with Mayakovsky was decisive. He saw himself moving as far as possible away from Futurism with its vulgarity, ostentation, and primitive violence. The Futurists were making public statements; he would go deeper and deeper within himself. They had broken with tradition and employed a language without roots, with a contrived and artificial bluntness; he would set himself squarely within the tradition. The Futurists wanted the violent overthrow of the government; he wanted a humane government calmly responsible to the people. The estrangement from Mayakovsky had been growing over the years, though outwardly they remained friends. The turning point had come. Pasternak resolved to write the poetry that was in him and to remove himself completely from the world of manifestos and literary cults. He foresaw that his poems might never be published and that he might lose one by one his remaining literary friends, but he was certain that he had chosen the right way.

As a poet he was then little known. One volume of immature verses, *A Twin in the Clouds,* had been published in 1914 on a private press owned by a group of young writers. There was a favorable introduction by the critic Nikolai Aseyev; the small book was elegantly bound, and the typography was exquisite. The poems, however, were disastrous, and Maria Baltrushaitis, the wife of the poet Jurgis Baltrushaitis, warned him that he would regret their publication. Pasternak later realized the justice of her warning and became ashamed of them.

His second book, *Over the Barriers,* was no better. It appeared not long after his arrival in Moscow. Many of the poems were mood pieces written deliberately about places: Venice, Marburg, railroad stations, rivers. In the poem on Marburg he noted that Martin Luther and the brothers Grimm had lived there. The poem, which grew out of his brief stay at Marburg University, showed that he had failed to capture the mood of the city. Some verses derive from Swinburne, whose troubling presence can be detected in many of Pasternak's early poems. *Over the Barriers,* which contains fifty poems written in 1915 and 1916, demonstrated a failure in talent which might have turned him away from poetry. Mayakovsky claimed to like them; Pasternak himself came in time to regard them as failures, and he would occasionally attempt to reshape and revise them. He had written *A Twin in the Clouds* while sitting dangerously in the branches of an old birch tree on his father's country estate, and he seems to have written *Over the Barriers* while poring over maps and a dictionary of human emotions. He had come to a dead end.

The summer of 1917 was unlike any summer the Russians had ever lived through. It was a period of chaotic improvisations, of thrusts and counterthrusts, of explosive violence and sudden calm. Conspiracies abounded. The Revolution had made everyone drunk, and people were astonished to discover that they could be drunk for so long. In St. Petersburg the Soviet of Workers' and Soldiers' Deputies challenged the power of the Provisional Government. Kerensky ruled by executive order, but his orders were not always obeyed. With the failure of the Kerensky offensive against the Germans in July and the simultaneous failure of Lenin's attempted coup d'état, it seemed that both Kerensky and Lenin were about to be destroyed, or at least to vanish from the pages of history. But in fact no new leaders appeared, and until the October Revolution they remained in command of the stage.

In that feverish summer Pasternak wrote most of the poems which appear in *Sister My Life*. Outwardly they have very little to do with the times. They are concerned with a love affair, a brief journey to the Urals, the exploration of private sensations. He finds his images in gardens, in mirrors, in colors. There are no slogans, no calls to arms. He was writing poetry as though divorced entirely from the world of events, entering deeper and deeper into himself, losing himself in a world of sensations; and the more he lost himself, the more vividly he recreated the atmosphere of his time. They are poems filled with the electric excitement of those days. The dam had burst. He wrote with a new urgency, as though his life depended upon it. The callow poet of *A Twin in the Clouds* and *Over the Barriers* had given place to a poet with a new, exciting, and memorable voice.

In the past Pasternak had set himself deliberately to write poetry on a chosen theme, building the stage furniture and simultaneously acting out the roles and performing as master of ceremonies. The backcloth would be painted with a river, a city, or a railroad yard, and the poem would be contained within a formal framework of studied elegance. He would attempt to imitate the noises of the railway yard, describe the city against the sunset, and find some surprising image which would suggest the exact texture of the light on the river. It was not difficult, and was neither rewarding nor particularly readable. What would happen if he threw all the stage properties away, abandoned the fashionable locutions of the time, surrendered to his own impulses and simply spoke with his own voice?

It was not perhaps a decision which he made consciously, although there is some evidence that he knew exactly what was happening. He was aware that he had failed to prove himself as a poet, and that drastic measures were needed. It was a question of survival, for he could only imagine himself as a poet and he had already failed in the three careers he had attempted. When he looked back on those times, he would say that he had been seized by a power "immeasurably greater than myself and the poetical ideas which then surrounded me." He also said that he was "entirely indifferent" to the nature of that power. But men are rarely indifferent to the power that grips them by the throat, and in time he became fully aware of it. He explained the process more fully in a famous passage in *Doctor Zhivago:*

After writing some verses which poured out easily and finding some images which pleasantly surprised him, he saw that the work had taken possession of him and he knew he was on the threshold of what is known as inspiration. The correlation of forces which determine a work of art seemed to be reversed. The dominant power no longer rested with the human being or the mood he was seeking to express, but with the language, his instrument of expression. Language, the home and container of beauty and meaning, itself begins to think and speak for man and turns wholly into music, not in the sense of outward and audible sound, but in the sense of the impetuosity and momentum of its inward flow. Then like the current of a mighty river, which polishes stones and turns waterwheels by its very movement, the flowing speech itself creates in its passage, by the force of its own laws, rhyme, meter and rhythm, and a thousand other forms and relationships even more important, as yet unexplored, unrecognized and unnamed.

At such moments Yury Andreyevich recognized that the greater part of the work was not being done by him, but by something which he knew to be above him, commanding him, and this was the thought and poetry of the world as it was now and as it would be in the future, inducing him to follow step by step in the order of its historical development. And he felt himself to be only the pretext, the fulcrum which would set it in motion.

Such was Pasternak's interpretation of the sudden alteration in his poetry which occurred in the summer of 1917, written many years after the event. If it is not entirely convincing, this is not due to any lack of scruple on Pasternak's part. He was speaking about things which are almost beyond the range of speech: the power of language to think its own thoughts, the great world reservoir of ideas and images, and the way language imposes itself on history. But when he spoke of the mighty river whose voice was so loud that it cannot be heard, and of language as "the home and container of beauty and meaning," then he was speaking in communicable terms. He believed, and often repeated, that in the rush and fury of emotion the words will find themselves. A poet did not compose a poem. Instead he called upon the poem to speak, summoning it out of the darkness into the light. For Pasternak poetry was not an avocation. It was the song sung by the universe, and it was the poet's task to throw a net across the heavens to capture it.

So it came about in that summer that he came to write poetry in a way which was so personal, so fresh, so shot through with colors which had never appeared in poetry before, that he seemed to be writing in a language which had not existed before. Occasionally he would write straightforwardly in recognizable Russian:

> Let the words fall
> Like a garden — amber and lemon peel,
> Bountifully seeded and scattered —

but more often he would speak in spells and riddles, which at first baffled the reader, sending him in search of the key, until he realized that no key was necessary. Pasternak had already writteen four poems on rivers when he wrote about the Shelon River:

> A face of azure gleams above the face
> Of his not-breathing and beloved river.
> A catfish stirs and starts.
> They are deaf; hear nothing; are far off.
>
> The eyes in the sheaves are as heavy as roofs,
> Like coals, with both hearths glowing.
> A face of azure gleams above the brow
> Of his not-breathing lady of the deep,
> Of his not-breathing nurseling of the marsh grass.
>
> The wind will carry the laughter of alfalfa
> Along the ridges, like blowing kisses,
> And regaling itself with the marshland's berries,
> It creeps along, smears its lips with the water fern,
> And flutters a branch on the river's cheek,
> Or sours and ferments among the reeds.

Do the perch's fins begin to throb —
The depthless day is huge and crimson;
The surface of the Shelon, black and leaden colored.
No ends to make meet and no hands to raise . . .

In this poem Pasternak was not so much depicting the mood of a river at nightfall as entering into it, becoming it, surrendering to its slow and delicate movement among the ferns and reeds. The effect is of an effortless and relentless music accompanying the mind and hands of the poet as they dip into the water, submerge and vanish, for only the river remains. That the river should finally become motionless, and therefore no longer a river, and that the sky should be "huge and crimson" and the river "black and leaden" only demonstrates what we already knew — that poetry inevitably involves paradox, and in the moment of vision all contraries are reconciled.

So in another poem Pasternak will speak of "a thunder eternally instantaneous," and the reader is left without any illusion that he meant exactly what he said. Throughout his life Pasternak was to be haunted by the accusation that he was the poet of paradox, deliberately creating dissonances in his imagery, but in fact the dissonances rise out of the nature of his intensely personal poetry, and though in later years he wrote in an increasingly dry and spare manner, saying that his early poems were artificial, there was nothing at all artificial in his way of looking at the world. He was the most emotional of poets. He would find himself at the mercy of wild enthusiasms, sudden elations, when the whole visible world would be lit by Bengal flares, and it was his task to capture those momentary visions. To capture the thunderstorms on the wing, the river in its flow, the raindrop as it hurls itself to the earth, and the leaping of the human heart — these things, which are almost beyond the power of human speech, were the subjects of his poems. He saw the world in suddennesses, and for him everything that happened was eternally instantaneous.

For such a poet there was never any need for artificial stimulation; he would never search for a theme; the world outside came racing into his window; and he was content that it should be so. He wrote about what he saw from his study table: a garden, fir trees, a fence, the falling snow. Somewhere there is a woman, but she rarely comes to disturb him, and she is rarely the same woman. On his occasional travels the railway train is so much a home to him that he will describe the compartment in minute detail. The sun, the rain, the thunderstorm are his familiars, and in his early poems he especially liked to describe the scents of summer and autumn in the changing weather. At heart he was always a countryman.

At the beginning of *Sister My Life* Pasternak made clear that he was not bound by any of the rules of the Symbolists and Futurists who had taken possession of Russian poetry. His loyalty was to Lermontov, the tragic poet of the early years of the nineteenth century, who insisted on the primacy of the senses. Sensual, arrogant, and intensely autobiographical, watching himself at all seasons, Lermontov lived out his brief life amid passionate intrigues and fiery adventures, which usually took place against the backdrop of the Caucasus mountains. Outwardly there was little in common between Pasternak and that dauntless Byronic figure, who lived according to an outmoded code of honor and died in a duel. A Russian poet writing in 1917 and claiming to be a follower of Lermontov could expect to be laughed out of court; the Symbolists and Futurists could hardly be expected to share his enthusiasm. Lermontov was *vieux jeu* and belonged to the remote antiquarian past. For Pasternak Lermontov was new. He was the poet who transformed his life into a perpetual celebration of the senses and knew himself so well that he could describe his emotions with brilliant accuracy. He was the first of the Russian confessional poets, and the most daring, for he held nothing back.

When Pasternak dedicated *Sister My Life* to Lermontov, he was proclaiming his independence from the current poetics of his age and at the same time affirming his belief in the validity of the tradition which passed through Lermontov and Tolstoy and culminated in Chekhov. There was an even more personal reason for the dedication. He wrote to a friend: "I dedicated *Sister My Life* not to the memory of Lermontov but to the poet himself as though he were living in our midst—to his spirit still effectual in our literature. What was he to me, you ask, in the summer of 1917? The personification of creative adventure and discovery, the principle of everyday free poetical statement." He was claiming for Lermontov the sovereign freedom he claimed for himself.

But where Lermontov moved outward, finding his images in mountains and soldiers, Pasternak moved just as furiously and relentlessly into the interior world, where the images might be as casual as a pair of lost spectacles or a mirror in the hall with a cup of cocoa standing on the mirror shelf. In one of the early poems in *Sister My Life*. he uses the image of the mirror with quite extraordinary effect:

> *On the shelf of the hall mirror, a steaming*
> > *Cup of cocoa rests. Satin sways;*
> *And — the mirror rushes out in a straight path*
> > *To the tumbledown chaos of swing and garden.*

> *There the pine trees prick the air*
> > *With their resin and their swaying;*
> *And absent-minded garden plots have mislaid*
> > *Spectacles on the grass; Shade reads a book.*

> *Further back, in the dark, beyond the fence*
> > *To the steppe, in the odor of opiates,*
> *And mixed with twigs and snails,*
> > *Flows a pathway of hot and glittering quartz.*

The enormous garden thrashes, harasses the mirror —
  And yet it does not shatter the glass!
Everything seems bathed in a gelatinous film
  From the mirror to the sound in the tree trunks.

And the mirror invasion has seemingly glazed
  Everything with unthawing ice,
Making the bitter branch tasteless; the lilac, scentless —
  Hypnosis could not be drowned out.

The all-pervasive peace minces in its mesmerism,
  And it is only the wind that causes it
To burst into life and break in the prism,
  And joyfully play in tears.

Do not blast out the soul like coal with nitro,
  Nor dig it out like a hidden treasure with spade.
The threatening garden thrashes, harasses the mirror —
  And yet it does not shatter the glass.

The mirror, of course, is the image of the poet himself,
drinking his cup of cocoa and gazing out at the unreach-
able world beyond. The wind-blown garden may be the
world, or a real garden, and the mirror itself is ice-cold
only because it resembles ice. The world seen in this mirror, like the world seen in a *camera oscura,* is not the
everyday world, but a more precise, detailed, and luminous
world colored by the poet's emotions, his passions, and
perhaps his yearning to smash the mirror and go out into
the wild garden.

In much the same way, with that concentrated luminous
gaze, Pasternak will describe a love affair, a railway journey, the flies buzzing around a teacup, black cherries staring out of their eye sockets, the milky foam rising out of a
piano as the hands play over the keys. Like a mirror the
poet remains silent and lets the images speak. If the images
are strange — we do not at first reconcile ourselves to black
cherries staring out of their eye sockets or the milky

foam rising out of a piano — we recognize their justice. These images, for Pasternak, are the language of the spirit. The world must be seen anew; otherwise it will perish.

This highly personal vision ultimately acquires impersonality, for we realize that he is speaking about the real world, even though it is a world we are not accustomed to. He is like a huntsman entering an enchanted forest, where the ghosts wander abroad and strange animals lurk in the undergrowth and there are signs reading: *Nur für Schwindelfrei* — Only for those who never suffer from vertigo. But in that enchanted forest he is at home, for he knows the pathways, the cave of the unicorns, and the tyrant's lair. Suddenly we realize that he is merely traveling through the familiar forest of the human soul, taking the unfamiliar pathways. There is a sense in which all his poems are descriptions of the soul at bay, caught in a shining light.

III

Pasternak completed *Sister My Life* in the autumn of 1917 and then put the poems away. A few copies were made and distributed among his friends; Mayakovsky approved of them, and Marina Tsvetaeva, who read them later, prophesied that Pasternak alone would come to wear the mantle of Pushkin, so deeply was she moved by them. But it was not a time propitious for poetry. He had scarcely finished the last poem when the October Revolution broke out. Pasternak neither welcomed nor deplored the Revolution. He regarded it as a natural phenomenon, like a thunderstorm: a few great trees would be struck by lightning, the river would flood its banks, devastations would be visited on the land, but the eternally instantaneous earth would soon revive.

It was an illusion shared by most of the poets of the time: the Revolution would pass and leave no more than a scar on the Russian earth. In time he would come to write poems in which he attempted to come to terms with the Revolution, but they were rarely successful. He attended one of the early meetings of the Petrograd Soviet when it was being addressed by Lenin, and he was impressed by the ferocious legendary power of that small redheaded man, who had only to raise his arm "and all history poured through his hands." The Revolution passed him by; he had no use for it, no need for its empty slogans and perilous promises. He made a living as a clerk in a bookshop. Later, through the influence of Mayakovsky, he was appointed a librarian in the Ministry of Education. These were times of poverty and misery, and he described them later in his long poem *The High Malady,* saying that he was "ashamed, every day more ashamed, that in an age of such shadows a certain high malady is still called song." In the summer of 1918 he wrote *The Childhood of Luvers,* the story of a young girl's growth into awareness. Not until he wrote *Doctor Zhivago* nearly forty years later did he write such powerful and delicate prose again. *The Childhood of Luvers* was a coda to *Sister My Life.* With that long short story he rounded off the experiences which went into his poems.

At last in 1922 *Sister My Life* appeared in print. That thin volume with a gray cover, impeccably printed on a Moscow press, announced the emergence of a major talent. To his surprise he became famous. Still more to his surprise, a whole generation of Russians grew up learning his poems by heart, so that on the rare occasions when he recited his poems in public and forgot his lines, the whole audience would thunder them back at him. In the days of Stalin's tyranny Russians took comfort from the fact that this tall, slender man with the bony, angular face continued to write poetry and miraculously survived all treacheries. He was one of those very rare poets who became a legend in their own time.

It was a legend which took root and flowered and extended far beyond the boundaries of Russia. There came a time when he no longer belonged to the Russian people alone, but to the whole world. If, as he believed, *Doctor Zhivago* was the summit of his achievement, *Sister My Life* first proclaimed his power over words and the delicacy of his enduring love affair with nature and with living things.

In these poems, so beautifully and sympathetically translated by Phillip Flayderman, we can see how it all began.

—*Robert Payne*

Оглавление

Contents

THE REPLACEMENT

SONGS IN LETTERS SO THAT SHE WON'T BE BORED

ROMANOVKA

AN ATTEMPT TO SEPARATE THE SOUL

THE RETURN

TO HELEN

EPILOGUE

THE END

ПОСВЯЩАЕТСЯ ЛЕРМОНТОВУ

Es braust der Wald, am Himmel zieh'n
Des Sturmes Donnerflüge;
Da mal' ich in das Wetter hin,
O Mädchen, deine Züge.

LENAU

TO LERMONTOV

The forest roars, across the sky
Sail stormy thunder clouds;
There, my dear, in the weather's din
I paint your lovely face.

                                        LENAU

СЕСТРА МОЯ ЖИЗНЬ

SISTER MY LIFE

Памяти Демона

Приходил по ночам
В синеве ледника от Тамары,
Парой крыл намечал,
Где гудеть, где кончаться кошмару.

Не рыдал, не сплетал
Оголенных, исхлестанных, в шрамах.
Уцелела плита
За оградой грузинского храма.

Как горбунья дурна,
Под решеткою тень не кривлялась.
У лампады зурна
Чуть дыша, о княжне не справлялась.

Но сверканье рвалось
В волосах и, как фосфор, трещали.
И не слышал колосс,
Как седеет Кавказ за печалью.

От окна на аршин,
Пробирая шерстинки бурнуса,
Клялся льдами вершин:
Спи, подруга, лавиной вернуся.

In Memory of the Demon[1]

He came at night from Tamara,[2]
In the frozen blue glare of the glacier,
Both wings marking the place
Where the howling was and the nightmare ended.

He did not weep, nor torment
The naked, the whipped ones wearing their scars.
There, behind the fence of a Georgian church,
One gravestone still survived.

Like an ugly hunchback, his shadow
Was unable to wiggle beneath the lattice.
Beside the icon lamp, a lute,
Barely breathing, unquestioning of its princess.

Yet a gleam of light raced through his hair,
Which trembled like phosphorus;
But Colossus did not hear
How the Caucasus grew gray in its sorrow.

A few feet from the window,
Plucking at the strands of his cloak,
He swore by the ice of the peaks:
"Beloved, sleep! I will return with the avalanche!"

НЕ ВРЕМЯ-ЛЬ ПТИЦАМ ПЕТЬ

ISN'T IT TIME
for the
BIRDS TO SING?

Про Эти Стихи

На троттуарах истолку
С стеклом и солнцем пополам,
Зимой открою потолку
И дам читать сырым углам.

Задекламирует чердак
С поклоном рамам и зиме,
К карнизам прянет чехарда
Чудачеств, бедствий и замет.

Буран не месяц будет месть,
Концы, начала заметет,
Внезапно вспомню: — солнце есть;
Увижу: свет давно не тот.

Галчонком глянет Рождество
И разгулявшийся денек
Прояснит много из того
Что мне и милой невдомек.

В кашне, ладонью заслонясь,
Сквозь фортку кликну детворе:
Какое, милые, у нас
Тысячелетье на дворе?

Кто тропку к двери проторил,
К дыре, засыпанной крупой,
Пока я с Байроном курил,
Пока я пил с Эдгаром По?

Пока в Дарьял, как к другу, вхож,
Как в ад, в цейхгауз, в арсенал,
Я жизнь, как Лермонтова дрожь,
Как губы, в вермут окунал.

About These Poems

Together I shall grind them with glass and sun
Into the streets; in winter
Speak them to the ceiling
And give damp corners a chance to read.

The garret will begin declaiming them
And curtsy to the winter window frames.
My game is leapfrog over eaves, mingling madness,
Grave disasters, pranks.

The storm will blow a month or more
And bury all beginnings, ends, in snow.
Then I will remember: There is a sun.
And I will see the world is not what it used to be.

Christmas will glare like a crow.
And clearing weather will clarify
A lot of things that never dawned
On my beloved or on me.

My muffled face protected by my hand,
I will shout across the windows to the children:
"Dear ones, can you tell me
What millennium you are celebrating out there?

"Who cleared that pathway to my door,
That hole all choked with sleet,
While I was smoking with Lord Byron
And drinking wine with Edgar Allan Poe?

"While I made my peace with Dáryal Pass,[3]
As with a friend, a trainyard, arsenal or hell —
And soaked my life, like lips
Or Lermontov's shudder, in vermouth."

[7]

Тоска

Для этой книги на эпиграф
Пустыни сипли,
Ревели львы и к зорям тигров
Тянулся Киплинг.

Зиял, иссякнув, страшный кладязь
Тоски отверстой,
Качались, ляская и гладясь
Иззябшей шерстью.

Теперь, качаться продолжая
В стихах вне ранга,
Бредут в туман росой лужаек
И снятся Гангу.

Рассвет холодною ехидной
Вползает в ямы,
И в джунглях сырость панихиды
И фимиама.

Ennui

Here is a motto for this book:
The howling wilderness, the lion's roar,
And Kipling stretching himself
For a dawn of tigers.

The dry and ghastly pit of boredom yawned;
And they were swinging,
Shivering and rubbing
Their frozen fur.

Now they continue to swing in verse.
Far beyond their reach. Raving
In misty clearings,
They dream of the Ganges.

With merciless envy, dawn crawls
Into their holes,
And in the jungle rises
A moist requiem and incense.

☆

Сестра моя жизнь и сегодня в разливе
Расшиблась весенним дождем обо всех,
Но люди в брелоках высоко брюзгливы
И вежливо жалят, как змеи в овсе.

У старших на это свои есть резоны.
Бесспорно, бесспорно смешон твой резон,
Что в грóзу лиловы глаза и газоны
И пахнет сырой резедой горизонт.

Что в мае, когда поездов расписанье
Камышинской веткой читаешь в купе,
Оно грандиозней святого писанья
И черных от пыли и бурь канапе.

Что только нарвется, разлаявшись, тормаз
На мирных сельчан в захолустном вине,
С матрацов глядят, не моя ли платформа,
И солнце, садясь, соболезнует мне.

И в третий плеснув, уплывает звоночек
Сплошным извиненьем: жалею, не здесь.
Под шторку несет обгорающей ночью
И рушится степь со ступенек к звезде.

Мигая, моргая, но спят где-то сладко
И фатаморганой любимая спит
Тем часом, как сердце, плеща по площадкам,
Вагонными дверцами сыплет в степи.

☆

Sister my life burst forth today
In torrents of spring rain, everywhere.
But people in jewels are highly squeamish
And bite politely, like hidden vipers.

The older people have their reasons for this;
And without doubt, your reason is confused:
That the lawn and those eyes are lilac in the storm
And the horizons smell of damp mignonettes;

So in May, riding in the compartment of a train,
You read the schedules of local railroads
And find them more impressive than Holy Scripture
Or coach seats black with dust and weather;

Or that the squealing of the brakes can rouse
The quiet peasants drunk with local wine.
They bolt from their mattresses: "Is this my station?"
While the setting sun is my sole consolation.

Third warning, and the bell swims past
With pure apology: "Sorry, not here."
The window shade descends on the dying sunset
And the steppe falls away between the footboard and the
        stars.

Winking and waking, someone still sleeps,
My beloved still sleeps like a lovely mirage,
Meanwhile my heart, splashing along the platform,
Strews carriage doors over the steppe.

Плачущий Сад

Ужасный! — Капнет и вслушается,
      Все он ли один на свете,
— Мнет ветку в окне, как кружевце, —
      Или есть свидетель.

Но давится внятно от тягости
      Отеков — земля ноздревая
И слышно: далеко, как в августе,
      Полуночь в полях назревает.

Ни звука. И нет соглядатаев.
      В пустынности удостоверясь,
Берется за старое — скатывается
      По кровле, за желоб, и через.

К губам поднесу, и прислушаюсь,
      Все я ли один на свете,
— Готовый навзрыд при случае, —
      Или есть свидетель.

Но тишь. И листок не шелохнется,
      Ни признака зги, кроме жутких
Глотков и плесканья в шлепанцах
      И вздохов и слез в промежутке.

The Weeping Garden

How horrible! It drips and listens,
  Is it then the only one in the world
That pushes the branch in at the window,
    Like a bit of lace in embroidery? Or someone *is*
      watching.

I hear the spongy earth.
    Weighed down by its own sogginess,
And listen: Far off, as in August,
    Midnight ripens in the fields.

No sounds; no secret watchers.
    Convinced it is alone, starts up again,
Rolling down the roof,
    Over and under gutters.

I will lift it to my lips and listen.
    Am I alone on earth?
Am I ready to weep for this?
    Or someone *is* watching.

Silence. Not a leaf stirs.
    No sign of light; only pathetic sobs
And scraping of slippers and sighing
    And tears in the pauses.

Зеркало

В трюмо испаряется чашка какао,
　　Качается тюль, и — прямой
Дорожкою в сад, в бурелом и хаос
　　К качелям бежит трюмо.

Там сосны враскачку воздух ссаднят
　　Смолой; там по маете
Очки по траве растерял палисадник,
　　Там книгу читает Тень.

И к заднему плану, во мрак, за калитку
　　В степь, в запах сонных лекарств
Струится дорожкой, в сучках и в улитках
　　Мерцающий, жаркий кварц.

Огромный сад тормошится в зале
　　В трюмо, — и не бьет стекла!
Казалось бы все коллодий залил
　　С комода до шума в стволах.

Зеркальная все б, казалось, нахлынь
　　Непотным льдом облила,
Чтоб сук не горчил и сирень не пахла
　　— Гипноза залить не могла.

Несметный мир семенит в месмеризме
　　И только ветру связать
Что ломится в жизнь и ломается в призме
　　И радо играть в слезах.

Души не взорвать, как селитрой залежь
　　Не вырыть, как заступом клад.
Огромный сад тормошится в зале
　　В трюмо, — и не бьет стекла.

The Mirror

On the shelf of the hall mirror, a steaming
    Cup of cocoa rests. Satin sways;
And — the mirror rushes out in a straight path
    To the tumbledown chaos of swing and garden.

There the pine trees prick the air
    With their resin and their swaying;
And absent-minded garden plots have mislaid
    Spectacles on the grass; Shade reads a book.

Further back, in the dark, beyond the fence
    To the steppe, in the odor of opiates,
And mixed with twigs and snails,
    Flows a pathway of hot and glittering quartz.

The enormous garden thrashes, harasses the mirror —
    And yet it does not shatter the glass!
Everything seems bathed in a gelatinous film
    From the mirror to the sound in the tree trunks.

And the mirror invasion has seemingly glazed
    Everything with unthawing ice,
Making the bitter branch tasteless; the lilac, scentless —
    Hypnosis could not be drowned out.

The all-pervasive peace minces in its mesmerism,
    And it is only the wind that causes it
To burst into life and break in the prism,
    And joyfully play in tears.

Do not blast out the soul like coal with nitro,
    Nor dig it out like a hidden treasure with spade.
The threatening garden thrashes, harasses the mirror —
    And yet it does not shatter the glass.

И вот, в гипнотической этой отчизне
Ничем мне очей не задуть.
Так после дождя проползают слизни
Глазами статуй в саду.

Шуршит вода по ушам и, чирикнув,
На цыпочках скачет чиж.
Ты можешь им выпачкать губы черникой,
Их шалостью не опоишь.

Огромный сад тормошится в зале,
Подносит к трюмо кулак,
Бежит на качели, ловит, салит,
Трясет и не бьет стекла!

And look, in this native land of hypnosis,
    I cannot blow out my sight.
Thus, after rain, do slugs crawl
    Over the eyes of garden statues.

Water rustles in my ears; and chirping,
    The siskin skips away on tiptoe.
You can stain their mouths with blueberries,
    But you cannot give them too many pranks to drink.

The enormous garden harasses the mirror,
    Raises its fist to the surface,
Runs to the swing, seizes it,
    Tags it wags it — but does not shatter the glass!

Девочка

*Ночевала тучка золотая
На груди утеса великана.*

Из сада, с качелей, с бухты-барахты
    Вбегает ветка в трюмо!
Огромная, близкая, с каплей смарагда
    На кончике кисти прямой.

Сад застлан, пропал за ее беспорядком,
    За бьющей в лицо кутерьмой
Родная, громадная, с сад, а — характером
    — Сестра! Второе трюмо!

Но вот эту ветку вносят в рюмке
    И ставят к раме трюмо.
Кто это — гадает, — глаза мне рюмит
    Тюремной людской дремой?

A Girl

A golden cloud spent the night
In the lap of a giant cliff.

LERMONTOV

From the garden, the seesaw, helter-skelter.
    A branch runs into the hall mirror,
A huge branch with a drop of emerald
    At the end of an arrow-straight tip.

The garden, disorderly and forgotten, decayed;
    The confusion stares you in the face.
Beloved, great one — by nature,
    Sister! Second mirror!

Someone will put this branch in a wine glass
    And place it near the frame of the mirror.
It wonders: "Who blurs my eyes
    With this prison pallor, this human stupor?"

☆

Ты в ветре, веткой пробующем,
Не время-ль птицам петь,
Намокшая воробушком
Сиреневая ветвь!

У капель — тяжесть запонок,
И сад слепит как плес,
Обрызганный, закапанный
Миллионом синих слез.

Моей тоскою выняньчен
И от тебя в шипах,
Он ожил ночью нынешней,
Забормотал, запа́х.

Всю ночь в окошко торкался,
И ставень дребезжал,
Вдруг дух сырой прогорклости
По платью пробежал.

Разбужен чудным перечнем
Тех прозвищ и времен,
Обводит день теперешний
Глазами анемон.

☆

Hey, you in the wind, beating your path
Through the branches, isn't it time for the birds to sing?
Yes, you, lilac branch, I mean,
Wet as a tiny sparrow.

The rain is as heavy as cuff links,
And the garden is blinding
As a lake dappled and dotted
By a million blue tears.

Nursed to health by my grief,
And because of you now covered with thorns,
The garden revived last night,
Gave off its fragrance, murmured.

All night it had tumbled about at my window
And hammered at the shutters.
Suddenly, the smell of rancid dampness
Ran along the clothes.

Awakened by the sudden roll call
Of those sobriquets and centuries,
Today's day looks about
With the eyes of anemones.

Дождь

Надпись на «Книге степи».

Она со мной. Наигрывай,
Лей, смейся, сумрак рви,
Топи, теки эпиграфом
К такой, как ты, любви!

Снуй шелкопрядом тутовым
И бейся об окно.
Окутывай, опутывай,
Еще не всклянь темно!

— Ночь в полдень, ливень, — гребень ей!
На щебне, взмок — возьми!
И — целыми деревьями
В глаза, в виски, в жасмин!

Осанна тьме Египетской!
Хохочут, сшиблись, — ниц!
И вдруг пахнуло выпиской
Из тысячи больниц.

Теперь бежим сощипывать,
Как стон со ста гитар,
Омытый мглою липовой
Садовый Сен-Готард.

Rain

She is with me. Play a tune,
Laugh, pour, rip at the half-dark!
Drown it, flow like an inscription
To that love which is you!

Scurry about like a silkworm
And knock on the window!
Muffle, enmesh in the dark
Whatever is yet untousled.

Night at noon! A cloudburst!
Crest of a wave rises to her! Throw your water
On the gravel, and by whole treefuls
Into the eyes, the temples, into the jasmine!

Hosanna to the Egyptian darkness!
They split with laughter; things tumble about — DOWN!
All of a sudden it smells like a prescription
From a thousand hospitals.

Now let us run and pinch together,
Like the groan from a hundred guitars,
A gardenlike St. Gothard
Washed in the lime-tree haze.

[23]

Книга Степи

Est-il possible, — le fût-il?
VERLAINE

ПЕРВАЯ ГЛАВА

Book of the Steppe

Is it possible — was it so?
VERLAINE

CHAPTER ONE

До Всего Этого Была Зима

В занавесках кружевных
Воронье.
Ужас стужи уж и в них
Заронен.

Это кружится октябрь,
Это жуть
Подобралась на когтях
К этажу.

Что ни просьба, что ни стон,
То, кряхтя,
Заступаются шестом
За октябрь.

Ветер за руки схватив,
Дерева
Гонят лестницей с квартир
По дрова.

Снег валится, и с колен
— В магазин
С восклицаньем: Сколько лет,
Сколько зим!

Сколько раз он рыт и бит,
Сколько им
Сыпан зимами с копыт
Кокаин!

Мокрой солью с облаков
И с удил
Боль, как пятна с башлыков,
Выводил.

Before This There Was Only Winter

In the lacy curtains,
There are ravens.
The horror of the hoarfrost
Hovers in them.

This is the whirling of October,
This, the terror,
Comes creeping on claws
Through the rooms of the house.

Every prayer and groan
Is cawing
That pleads in unison
For October.

Seizing the wind by the hands,
The trees chase
Down the stairs from the house
To the woodpile.

Snow comes in flurries and rushes
Knee-deep into the shop
Shouting, "How many years?
How many winters!"

How many times was the snow pitted and beaten!
How much cocaine
Was poured from its frozen hooves
In winter!

Like damp salt from clouds
Or a horse's foaming bit,
The snow expunged pain
As if it were stains on winter hoods.

Из Суеверья

Коробка с красным померанцем —
    Моя каморка.
О, не об номера ж мараться
    По гроб, до морга!

Я поселился здесь вторично
    Из суеверья.
Обоев цвет, как дуб, коричнев
    И — пенье двери.

Из рук не выпускал защелки,
    Ты вырывалась,
И чуб касался чудной чолки
    И губы — фиалок.

О, неженка, во имя прежних
    И в этот раз твой
Наряд щебечет, как подснежник
    Апрелю: здравствуй!

Грех думать, ты не из весталок:
    Вошла со стулом,
Как с полки, жизнь мою достала
    И пыль обдула.

Out of Superstition

My hotel room is like a box of russet,
  Bitter oranges.
O, be careful, do not get soiled as you go
  Coffined to the morgue.

I settled here a second time
  Out of superstition.
The wallpaper is brown as oak —
  And the singing of the door!

My hand was still upon the latch,
  You were struggling to get out.
My forelock touched your fearful forehead.
  Your lips were violets.

My dear, in the name of times gone by,
  Your dress chirps this time, too.
Like a snowdrop to April:
  "Hello!"

It is a sin to think you are not a vestal virgin
  You walked in with a chair,
Handed me life from the shelf,
  And blew the dust away.

Не Трогать

«Не трогать, свеже выкрашен», —
    Душа не береглась,
И память — в пятнах икр и щек
    И рук и губ и глаз.

Я больше всех удач и бед
    За то тебя любил,
Что пожелтелый белый свет
    С тобой — белей белил.

И мгла моя, мой друг, божусь,
    Он станет как-нибудь
Белей, чем бред, чем абажур,
    Чем белый бинт на лбу!

Don't Touch

"Wet Paint! Don't Touch!"
        My heart never heeded —
And memory is now a stain of legs,
        Cheeks, hands, ankles, lips, eyes.

Better than all success or sorrow
        I loved you because with you
The jaundiced world grew brighter
        Brighter than zinc white.

And darkness, my friend, I swear
        Will somehow become
Whiter than madness, than a lampshade,
        Than my bandaged brow.

☆

Ты так играла эту роль!
Я забывал, что сам — суфлер,
Что будешь петь и во второй,
Кто б первой ни совлек.

Вдоль облаков шла лодка. Вдоль
Лугами кошеных кормов.
Ты так играла эту роль,
Как лепет шлюз — кормой!

И, низко рея на руле
Касаткой об одном крыле,
Ты так — ты лучше всех ролей
Играла эту роль!

O, how you played this role!
I forgot that I myself was prompter,
And that you would sing in the second act —
You who had not yet rung down the first.

Among the clouds, a drifting boat,
Among the fields of high-mown hay,
O, how you played this role
Like the foaming wake at the stern!

And hovering over the rudder,
Like a swallow tipped on one wing —
Yes, that was you, and you played this role
Better than all the others.

Балашов

По будням медник подле вас
Клепал, лудил, паял,
А впрочем — масла подливал
В огонь, как пай к паям.

И без того душило грудь
И песнь небес: «твоя, твоя»
И без того лилась в жару
В вагон, на саквояж.

Сквозь дождик сеялся хорал
На гроб и в шляпы молокан,
А впрочем — ельник подбирал
К прощальным облакам.

И без того взошел, зашел
В больной душе, щемя, мечась,
Большой, как солнце, Балашов
В осенний ранний час.

Лазурью июльскою облит,
Базар синел и дребезжал,
Юродствующий инвалид
Пиле, гундося, подражал.

Мой друг, ты спросишь, кто велит,
Чтоб жглась юродивого речь?
В природе лип, в природе плит,
В природе лета было жечь.

Balashov[4]

On workdays, the tinker at your side
Riveted, tinned, and patched,
While pouring all the while
Fuel on the fire like compound interest.

And for all that his heart was choked,
His heavenly song, "Yours, only yours!"
He poured it on the parching heat,
The train and traveling bag.

The dirge was sown across the gentle rain,
On the coffins and mourners' hats,
While spruce groves tossed it up
To valedictory clouds.

Nevertheless, it rose and climbed around,
The sick heart aching and tossing,
A giant like the sun, Balashov,
In early autumn hours.

Melting with July's hot haze,
The bazaar turned blue and softly tinkled.
God's fool was ill, and
Mimicked the groan of a saw.

My friend, you ask by whose command
The words of God's fool are burned?
In a world of lindens, a world of tombstones,
A world of summers — there was the fire.

Подражатели

Пекло, и берег был высок.
С подплывшей лодки цепь упала
Змеей гремучею — в песок,
Гремучей ржавчиной — в купаву.

И вышли двое. Под обрыв
Хотелось крикнуть им: простите,
Но бросьтесь, будьте так добры́,
Не врозь, так в реку, как хотите.

Вы верны лучшим образцам.
Конечно, ищущий обрящет,
Но... бросьте лодкою бряцать:
В траве терзается образчик.

Imitators

Scorching heat. The bank was high.
A boat sailed up. The chain
Shot into weeds and sand,
A rattling snake of grit and rust.

Two got out. Under the cliff,
I almost shouted, "Say,
Be so kind and spring
Headlong in the water!

"You're true to even better models,
And as they say, 'The seeker finds.'
I beg you, stop bobbing in your boat;
Your counterpart on land resents it."

Образец

О, бедный Homo Sapiens,
    Существованье — гнет.
Былые годы за пояс
    Один такой заткнет.

Все жили в сушь и впроголодь,
    В борьбе ожесточась,
И никого не трогало,
    Что чудо жизни — с час.

С тех рук впивавши ландыши,
    На те глаза дышав,
Из ночи в ночь валандавшись,
    Гормя горит душа.

Одна из южных мазанок
    Была других южней,
И ползала, как пасынок,
    Трава в ногах у ней.

Сушился холст. Бросается
    Еще сейчас к груди
Плетень в ночной красавице,
    Хоть год и позади.

Он незабвенен тем еще,
    Что пылью припухал,
Что ветер лускал семечки,
    Сорил по лопухам.

Что незнакомой мальвою
    Вел, как слепца, меня,
Чтоб я тебя вымаливал
    У каждого плетня.

A Specimen

I pity you, *homo sapiens,*
    Your life is pain;
Only few outsmart
    The ravages of time.

Everyone lived in drought and dearth,
    Growing more bitter in the battle.
But no one cared
    That life's wonder was but an hour.

I drank lily of the valley from her hands
    And breathed upon her eyes.
From night to night, I loitered at her door,
    My mind and heart ablaze.

One of the southern mud-walled huts
    Was more southern than the rest;
The grass crept along its walls
    Like a stepson at her feet.

The artist's canvas now is dry,
    And yet my heart is still afire
With braids of a night beauty,
    Although it was a year ago.

And still I have not forgotten
    The wind puffed up with dust
Scattering sunflower seeds,
    Squandering them on the burdock.

It led me like a blind man
    Through unfamiliar hollyhocks
So that I begged for you in my dreams
    By every wattle fence.

[39]

Сошел и стал окидывать
 Тех новых луж масла,
Разбег тех рощ ракитовых,
 Куда я письма слал.

Мой поезд только тронулся.
 Еще вокзал, Москва,
Плясали в кольцах, в конусах
 По насыпи, по рвам.

А уж гудели кобзами
 Колодцы, и, пылясь,
Скрипели, бились об землю
 Скирды и тополя.

Пусть жизнью связи портятся,
 Пусть гордость ум вредит,
Но мы умрем со спертостью
 Тех розысков в груди.

It came down, and its glance
      Swept over the new daubs of paint,
Ran down among the willow groves
      Where I sent many a letter.

My train has barely moved —
      And still the Moscow station —
There is dancing in rings and crowds,
      Along the banks and canals.

Already the wells whistled
      Like ancient Ukrainian lutes,
Hayricks and poplars making dust
      Roared and beat the ground.

Let the bonds be frayed by life!
      Let pride despoil our wit!
We shall die with those questions
      Stifled in our hearts.

РАЗВЛЕЧЕНЬЯ ЛЮБИМОЙ

AMUSEMENTS
of the
BELOVED

Душистою веткою машучи,
    Впивая впотьмах это благо,
Бежала на чашечку с чашечки
    Грозой одуренная влага.

На чашечку с чашечки скатываясь,
    Скользнула по двум, и в обеих
Огромною каплей агатовою
    Повисла, сверкает, робеет.

Пусть ветер по таволге веющий,
    Ту капельку мучит и плющит,
Цела, не дробится, — их две еще
    Целующихся и пьющих.

Смеются и вырваться силятся
    И выпрямиться, как прежде,
Да капле из рылец не вылиться,
    И не разлучатся, хоть режьте.

☆

Swaying on a scented branch,
    Drinking in the dark this bliss,
A raindrop, dazed by thunder,
    Ran from flower cup to flower cup.

Gliding from cup to cup,
    It slid smoothly along two flowers,
In both a great drop of agate
    Hung there, glistening shyly.

Let the wind blowing over the meadow
    Torture and flatten that raindrop.
It is whole and will not be divided;
    The two of them kissing and drinking.

They laugh and prepare to separate,
    To straighten up as before.
But the raindrop will not pour down the stamen,
    And cannot be separated, even by cutting.

Сложа Весла

Лодка колотится в сонной груди,
Ивы нависли, целуют в ключицы,
В локти, в уключины — о, погоди,
Это ведь может со всяким случиться!

Этим ведь в песне тешатся все.
Это ведь значит пепел сиреневый,
Роскошь крошеной ромашки в росе,
Губы и губы на звезды выменивать!

Это ведь значит обнять небосвод,
Руки сплести вкруг Геракла громадного,
Это ведь значит века напролет,
Ночи на щелканье славок проматывать!

Oars at Rest

A boat knocks at a sleepy breast,
The willows hang, kissing their collarbones,
Their elbows, oarlocks.
Just wait! This can happen to anyone.

Everyone rejoices in this song,
By which I mean the lilac ashes,
The splendor of crushed daisies in dew
Exchanging every lip for a star.

It is embracing the heavens;
Clasping hands around a giant Hercules;
Whole centuries of squandering
Nights on the songs of nightingales.

Весенний Дождь

Усмехнулся черемухе, всхлипнул, смочил
Лак экипажей, деревьев трепет.
Под луною на выкате, гуськом, скрипачи
Пробираются к театру. Граждане, в цепи!

Лужи на камне. Как полное слез
Горло, — глубокие розы, в жгучих
Влажных алмазах. Мокрый нахлест
Счастья — на них, на ресницах, на тучах.

Впервые луна эти цепи и трепет
Платьев и власть восхищенных уст,
Гипсовою эпопеею лепит,
Лепит никем не лепленный бюст.

В чьем это сердце вся кровь его быстро
Хлынула к славе, схлынув со щек?
Вон она бьется: руки министра
Рты и аорты сжали в пучок.

Это не ночь, не дождь и не хором
Рвущееся: «Ке — ренский, ура!»,
Это слепящий выход на форум
Из катакомб, безысходных вчера.

Это не розы, не рты, не ропот
Толп, это здесь, перед театром — прибой,
Заколебавшейся ночи Европы,
Гордой на наших асфальтах собой.

Spring Rain

The rain laughed at the bird cherries,
Wept and splattered the lacquered carriages,
Shook the trees. Musicians beneath the wide-eyed moon
File into the theater. Citizens, line up!

Rain pools on the stones. Like a throat
Full of tears, the deep roses
In burning wet diamonds.
A splash of joy on them, on eyelashes, on clouds.

These early queues and fluttering dresses,
Power of enraptured lips shaped into epics,
Are sculpted in the moon's plaster light
Into shapes never made before.

In whose heart did the blood first rush quickly
Coloring the cheeks with glory?
Look! It beats. The hands of the Minister
Squeezed mouths and aortas tight in his grasp.

No night, no rain, no roaring chorus
Broke out the words: "Ke-rensky,[5] Hurrah!"
This blinding escape from catacombs,
Yesterday's place of no exit, into public debate.

This is not roses, not lips, not roaring
Of crowds; but here in front of the theater —
These are the waves of Europe's unresting night,
Exultant on our asphalt streets.

Свистки Милиционеров

Дворня бастует. Брезгуя
Мусором пыльным и тусклым,
Ночи сигают до брезгу
Через заборы на мускулах.

Возятся в вязах, падают,
Не удержавшись, с деревьев,
Вскакивают: за оградою
Север злодейств сереет.

И вдруг, из садов, где твой
Лишь глаз ночевал, из милого
Душе твоей мрака, — плотвой
Свисток расплескавшийся выловлен.

Милиционером зажат
В кулак, как он дергает жабрами,
И горлом, и глазом, назад,
По рыбьи, наискось задранным!

Трепещущего серебра
Пронзительная горошина,
Как утро бодряще мокра
Звездой за забор переброшена.

И там, где тускнеет восток
Чахоткою летнего Тиволи,
Валяется дохлый свисток,
В пыли агонической вывалян.

Gendarme's Whistles

The servants go out on strike.
Shrinking from the dusty tarnished sweepings
They dawdle away the night in boredom
And leap over the fences.

They climb up the elms and fall,
Losing their hold, from the trees.
They leap over the side of the fence.
The North, with its evil designs, turns gray.

All of a sudden, there comes from the garden,
Where only your eyes spent the night,
Out of the darkness sweet to your soul
A whistle, like a carp splashing, pulled out of the water.

So, clutched in the policeman's fists,
O, how he shakes his gills,
And his throat and eyes, back and forth
In fish fashion.

The shrill sweet pea, trembling silver,
Like the morning cheering up
On a wet damp day, the whistle,
Falls across the fence like a star.

And there, where the eastern sky
Grows dim like the tubercular summer in Tivoli,[6]
The dead whistle wallows about,
Tumbled in the agonized dust.

Звезды Летом

Рассказали страшное,
Дали точный адрес.
Отпирают, спрашивают,
Движутся, как в театре.

Тишина, ты — лучшее
Из всего, что слышал.
Некоторых мучает,
Что летают мыши.

Июльской ночью слободы —
Чудно белокуры.
Небо в бездне поводов,
Чтоб набедокурить.

Блещут, дышут радостью,
Обдают сияньем,
На таком-то градусе
И меридиане.

Ветер розу пробует
Приподнять, по просьбе
Губ, волос и обуви,
Подолов и прозвищ.

Газовые, жаркие,
Осыпают в гравий
Все, что им нашаркали,
Все, что наиграли.

Summer Stars

They told a terrible tale
And gave the right address.
The door is opened, questions asked.
People move as on a stage.

Silence, you are better than all
I ever heard. Some people
Are quite disturbed
By bats that fly.

The suburbs on a July night
Are wonderfully white.
The sky is bottomless causes
To be playing pranks.

They glitter, breathe their joy,
They splash with their gleaming,
At a certain longitude
And latitude.

The breeze attempts to lift a rose
At the request of locks,
Lips, boots, hems,
And nicknames.

But they, gaseous, hot,
Scatter in gravel
Everything patched together,
Everything played to the heart's content.

Когда случилось петь Дездемоне,
— А жить так мало оставалось, —
Не по любви, своей звезде она, —
По иве, иве разрыдалась.

Когда случилось петь Дездемоне
И голос завела, крепясь,
Про черный день, чернейший демон ей
Псалом плакучих русл припас.

Когда случилось петь Офелии,
— А жить так мало оставалось, —
Всю сушь души взмело и свеяло,
Как в бурю стебли с сеновала.

Когда случилось петь Офелии,
А горечь грез осточертела,
С какими канула трофеями?
С охапкой верб и чистотела.

Дав страсти с плеч отлечь, как рубищу,
Входили, с сердца замираньем,
В бассейн вселенной, стан свой любящий
Обдать и оглушить мирами.

English Lessons

When Desdemona's time for singing came —
So little time was left for her to live —
She sang of willows, not of love, her star;
Willow, willow, came her heartbroken song.

When Desdemona's time for singing came,
In agony she sang of her dark hour,
A darkest demon lay in store for her
A psalm of weeping river beds.

When Ophelia's time for singing came —
So little time was left for her to live —
Then her parched soul was tossed in the air
Like stalks of straw from hayricks in a storm.

When Ophelia's time for singing came,
From bitter dreams was banished all restraint.
What trophies did she take into her grave?
A spray of willows and some celandine.

Their passions, like old clothes, swept off their shoulders,
So they entered, hearts sinking,
Into the reservoir of the universe:
Their images will drench and deafen all the world.

ЗАНЯТЬЯ
ФИЛОСОФИЕЙ

OCCUPATIONS
OF PHILOSOPHY

Определенье Поэзии

Это — круто налившийся свист,
Это — щелканье сдавленных льдинок,
Это — ночь, леденящая лист,
Это — двух соловьев поединок.

Это — сладкий, заглохший горох,
Это — слезы вселенной в лопатках,
Это — с пультов и с флейт — Figaro
Низвергается градом на грядку.

Все, что ночи так важно сыскать
На глубоких купаленных доньях,
И звезду донести до садка,
На трепещущих, мокрых ладонях.

Площе досок в воде — духота.
Небосвод завалился ольхою.
Этим звездам к лицу-б хохотать,
Ан вселенная — место глухое.

Definition of Poetry

A steeply crescendoing whistle.
A ringing of icicles knocked together.
A night that freezes the leaves.
A duel between nightingales.

A sweetpea run to seed.
A pod filled with the tears of the universe.
A fluteful of Figaro
Dashed down like hail on flowerbeds.

It is everything important night can reveal
In the depths of swimming holes. It is
Carrying a star to the garden
On damp, trembling palms.

Flatter than planks in water; sultry heat.
The firmament crammed full of alders;
It would become the stars to laugh,
But the universe is a murky place.

Определенье Души

Спелой грушею в бурю слететь
Об одном безраздельном листе.
Как он предан, — расстался с суком!
Сумасброд, — задохнется в сухом!

Спелой грушею, ветра косей.
Как он предан, — меня не затреплет,
Оглянись: — отгремела в красе,
Отпылала, осыпалась, — в пепле.

Нашу родину буря сожгла.
Узнаешь ли гнездо свое, птенчик?
О мой лист, ты пугливей щегла!
Что ты бьешься, о шелк мой застенчивый?

О, не бойся, приросшая песнь!
И куда порываться еще нам?
Ах, наречье смертельное «здесь» —
Невдомек содроганью сращенному.

Definition of the Soul

To fly off like a ripe pear in a storm,
For the sake of one inseparable leaf.
When leaving the branch, it was betrayed;
The fool, it will die in the dust.

Like a ripe pear athwart the wind,
How it was betrayed! "I'm not worried."
Look about you! The pear tumbled down in its beauty,
It flared up, crumbled, fell to ashes.

The storm set fire to our motherland.
Do you recognize your nest now, little chick?
Say, leaf, more frightened than a goldfinch,
Silken one, shy one, why do you struggle?

O, do not fear now, song that has grown strong!
Whither shall we run off to today?
Ah, that is a mortal adverb: "Here."
It never dawned on us huddled in shuddering.

Болезни Земли

О еще! — Раздастся-ль только хохот
Перламутром, Иматрой бацилл,
Мокрым гулом, тьмой стафилококков,
И блеснут при молниях резцы,

Так — шабаш! Нешаткие титаны
Захлебнутся в черных сводах дня,
Тени стянет трепетом tetanus
И медянок запылит столбняк.

Вот и ливень. Блеск водобоязни,
Вихрь, обрывки бешеной слюны.
Но откуда? С тучи, с поля, с Клязьмы
Или с сардонической сосны?

Чьи стихи настолько нашумели,
Что и гром их болью изумлен?
Надо быть в бреду по меньшей мере,
Чтобы дать согласье быть землей.

Diseases of the Earth

Again! Will only the mother-of-pearl
Laughter will be heard in cascades of bacilli,
Swarms of staphylococci, and with damp, distant rumble
Scissors spark out in the lightning?

Enough! Let these unshaking titans choke away
In their dark crypts of the microcosm.
Tetanus tightens the shadows with trembling;
Grass snakes, covered with dust, lie in stupor.

Here is a cloudburst for you: brilliance of hydrophobia,
Whirlwind, scraps of mad saliva.
But where does it all come from? Clouds, fields, river,
Or is it from sardonic pine trees?

Whose poems were so noisy
That even the thunder stood amazed?
You should at the very least be delirious
To agree to being on earth!

Определенье Творчества

Разметав отвороты рубашки,
Волосато, как торс у Бетховена,
Накрывает ладонью, как шашки,
Сон и совесть, и ночь, и любовь оно.

И какую-то черную до́ведь,
И — с тоскою какою-то бешеной,
К представлению света готовит,
Конноборцем над пешками пешими.

А в саду, где из погреба, со льду,
Звезды благоуханно разахались,
Соловьем над лозою Изольды
Захлебнулась Тристанова захолодь.

И сады, и пруды, и ограды,
И кипящее белыми воплями
Мирозданье — лишь страсти разряды,
Человеческим сердцем накопленной.

Definition of Creativity

Shirt open at the collar,
It is hairy as Beethoven's torso.
It covers conscience, dream, love, night
Like chessmen with its hand.

One black piece, made queen,
With a certain insane sadness,
It holds in reserve for daybreak
Threatening pawns with a knight.

But in the garden, where the stars
Fragrantly sighed from the ice-cellar,
Tristan's cold draught was drowned
Like a nightingale on Isolde's vine.

And gardens, ponds, parks,
The universe, boiling with white wailing,
Are all only salvos of passion
Hoarded in the human heart.

Наша Гроза

Гроза, как жрец, сожгла сирень
И дымом жертвенным застлала
Глаза и тучи. — Расправляй
Губами вывих муравья.

Звон ведер сшиблен набекрень.
О, что за жадность: неба мало?!
— В канаве бьется сто сердец.
Гроза сожгла сирень, как жрец.

В эмали — луг. Его лазурь,
Когда бы зябли, — соскоблили.
Но даже зяблик не спешит
Стряхнуть алмазный хмель с души.

У кадок пьют еще грозу
Из сладких шапок изобилья,
И клевер бурен и багров
В бордовых брызгах маляров.

К малине липнут комары.
Однако-ж, хобот малярийный,
Как раз сюда вот, изувер,
Где роскошь лета розовей?!

Сквозь блузу заронить нарыв
И сняться красной балериной?
Всадить стрекало озорства,
Где кровь, как мокрая листва?!

О верь игре моей, и верь
Гремящей вслед тебе мигрени!
Так гневу дня судьба гореть
Дичком в черешенной коре.

Our Thunderstorm

The storm, like a priest, set fire to the lilacs
And spread sacrificial smoke over
Eyes and clouds. Go heal
By lips alone the sprain of an ant.

The clatter of buckets knocked askew.
What greed! Not enough sky?
A ditch beats with a hundred hearts,
The storm, like a priest, set fire to the lilacs.

The meadow is all enamel;
Its frozen azure has been peeled off.
Even the finch is slow to shed
This diamond intoxication from the soul.

At drain tubs the storm is still on draft
By delightful hatfuls; and the clover,
Wild and crimson, the painters,
Speckled with claret.

Mosquitoes cling to raspberries.
The mosquito beak, that malarial madman,
Has its place just here.
Where else is the luxury of summer rosier?

He pricked through the blouse, causing a swelling,
Having inserted the blade of mischief
Into the blood moist like foliage,
And rose like a scarlet ballerina.

You had best believe my playing about —
Believe the thundering migraine in store for you.
Thus on the day of wrath, it is fated to burn
Like wild fruit on the cherry's bark.

[67]

Поверила? — теперь, теперь
Приблизь лицо, и в озареньи
Святого лета твоего,
Раздую я в пожар его!

Я от тебя не утаю:
Ты прячешь губы в снег жасмина,
— Я чую на моих тот снег,
Он тает на моих во сне.

Куда мне радость деть мою?
В стихи, в графленную осьмину?
— У них растрескались уста
От ядов писчего листа.

Они, с алфавитом в борьбе,
Горят румянцем на тебе.

ЭТИ РАЗВЛЕЧЕНЬЯ ПРЕКРАТИЛИСЬ, КОГДА, УЕЗЖАЯ, ОНА СДАЛА
СВОЮ МИССИЮ ЗАМЕСТИТЕЛЬНИЦЕ.

So, do you believe? Now, now,
Bring your face closer, and
In the shimmer of your holy summer,
I will fan it to a burst of flame.

I will not keep the truth from you:
You hide your lips in jasmine snow.
I feel the snow now with my lips;
On mine it melts in sleep.

Where shall I set down my joy?
In verses or in a ruled notebook?
Their lips are chapped and rough
With poisons of the written page.

They wage a war on the alphabet
And flush your cheeks in pure embarrassment.

THESE DIVERSIONS CAME TO AN END, WHEN, DEPARTING, SHE
CEDED HER MISSION TO THE REPLACEMENT.

ЗАМЕСТИТЕЛЬНИЦА

THE REPLACEMENT

☆

Я живу с твоей карточкой, с той, что хохочет,
У которой суставы в запястьях хрустят,
Той, что пальцы ломает и бросить не хочет,
У которой гостят, и гостят и грустят.

Что от треска колод, от бравады Ракочи,
От стекляшек в гостиной, от стекла и гостей
По пьянино в огне пробежится и вскочит
От розеток, костяшек и роз, и костей.

Чтоб прическу ослабив, и чайный и шалый,
Зачаженный бутон заколов за кушак,
Провальсировать к славе, шутя, полушалок
Закусивши, как муку, и еле дыша.

Чтобы комкая корку рукой, мандарина
Холодящие дольки глотать, торопясь
В опоясанный люстрой, позади за гардиной,
Зал, испариной вальса запахший опять.

Так сел бы вихрь, чтоб на пари
Порыв паров в пути
И мглу и иглы, как мюрид,
Не жмуря глаз снести.

И об'явить, что не скакун,
Не шалый шопот гор,
Но эти розы на боку
Несут во весь опор.

Не он, не он, не шопот гор,
Не он, не топ подков,
Но только то, но только то,
Что — стянута платком.

☆

I live with that photo of you, the one that laughs,
The one that snaps its wrist bones and
Keeps cracking its knuckles and will not give up.
The one people visit and visit and visibly grieve over.

The one filled with crackle of logs and Rakoczy marches,
With the tinkle of glasses, guests,
The tumblers and tippling. It bursts from the piano
With roses, rosettes, the dice, and the dicers.

Hair askew, you madly tucked
A rosebud under your waistband,
You waltzed to glory, joking,
Jesting, biting, twisting, barely breathing.

Tearing the rind in rings, you swallowed
The icy slices of tangerine, then ran back
Through portieres to the ballroom ablaze with light
And reeking of waltzes' sweat.

> This is how a blizzard descends,
> On a bet, blindly,
> Enduring dark and thorns like a Moslem
> Without batting an eye.

> You said you were no race horse
> Nor wild whisper of mountains.
> But those roses at your side
> Gallop by at a terrible speed!

> No, no, not the whisper of mountains;
> No, not the stamp of hooves.
> But merely, merely —
> What is caught by a handkerchief.

[73]

И только то, что тюль и ток,
Душа, кушак и в такт
Смерчу умчавшийся носок,
Несут, шумя в мечтах.

Им, им — и от души смеша,
И до упаду, в лоск,
На зависть мчащимся мешкам,
До слез, — до слез!

Only what is lacy and flowing,
Soul, waistband, whirling toes
Wheeling away to the tune of cyclones,
Vanishing loudly into dreams.

Yes, to them, to them — making them rock with
    laughter
To the point of falling,
Or blinding, or to the envy of whirling dolts
To tears — to tears.

ПЕСНИ В ПИСЬМАХ, ЧТОБЫ НЕ СКУЧАЛА

SONGS IN LETTERS
SO THAT
SHE WON'T BE BORED

Грудь под поцелуи, как под рукомойник!
Ведь не век, не сряду лето бьет ключем,
Ведь не ночь за ночью низкий рев гармоник
Подымаем с пыли, топчем и влечем.

Я слыхал про старость. — Страшны прорицанья!
Рук к звездам не вскинет ни один бурун.
Говорят, — не веришь: на лугах лица нет,
У прудов нет сердца, Бога нет в бору.

Расколышь же душу! Всю сегодня выпень.
Это полдень мира. Где глаза твои?
Видишь, в высях мысли сбились в белый кипень
Дятлов, туч и шишек, жара и хвои.

Здесь пресеклись рельсы городских трамваев.
Дальше служат сосны. Дальше им нельзя.
Дальше — воскресенье. Ветки отрывая,
Разбежится просек, по траве скользя.

Просевая полдень, Тройцын день, гулянье,
Просит роща верить: мир всегда таков.
Так задуман чащей, так внушен поляне,
Так на нас, на ситцы пролит с облаков.

Sparrow Hills[7]

Kisses on your breasts like water from an ewer;
But not forever, summer is no ever-flowing spring.
Nor shall we, night after night, raise up from the dust
The accordion's drone, stamping and pounding our feet.

I have heard about old age. Dreadful prophecy!
Not one crest of a wave will reach for the stars.
They say — you won't believe it — there is no face on the
      meadows;
In the pond, no heart; no god in the pine grove.

Set your soul rocking! Today all is frenzied:
This is the high noon of the world. Use your eyes! Look!
In the hilltops, thought is whipped to a white boiling
Of woodpeckers, clouds, heat, pine cones, and needles.

Here the rails of the city trolleys come to an end.
From there on the pine trees take their place —
The end of the line for machines. The beginning of Sunday.
A breaking of branches, a caper of clearings and sliding on
      grass.

Here, filtering sunlight, Whitsunday, walking about,
The woods beg belief: The world is always so!
This is the thought of the forest depth, the meadow's
      intimation;
Thus, on us, on colorful calico, it is poured from clouds.

По стене сбежали стрелки.
Час похож на таракана.
Брось, к чему швырять тарелки,
Бить тревогу, бить стаканы?

С этой дачею досчатой
Может и не то стрястися.
Счастье, счастью нет пощады!
Гром не грянул, что креститься?

Может молния ударить, —
Вспыхнет мокрою кабинкой.
Или всех щенят раздарят.
Дождь крыло пробьет дробинкой.

Все еще нам лес — передней,
Лунный жар за елью — печью,
Все, как стиранный передник,
Туча сохнет и лепечет.

И когда к колодцу рвется
Смерч тоски, то мимоходом
Буря хвалит домоводство
Что еще тебе угодно?

Год сгорел на керосине
Залетевшей в лампу мошкой,
Вон, зарею серо-синей,
Встал он сонный, встал намокший.

Он глядит в окно, как в дужку,
Старый, страшный состраданьем,
От него мокра подушка,
Он зарыл в нее рыданья.

Mein Liebchen, Was Willst Du Noch Mehr?

The clock hands have raced along the wall;
The hour is like a cockroach.
Stop! Why smash the plates,
Sound alarms, or shatter the glasses?

In this wooden country house,
Other things can be shaken away.
Happiness — there is no mercy for happiness!
It did not thunder. Why cross yourself?

Maybe lightning will strike —
It will flare up like a damp cabin.
Perhaps they will give away puppies.
The rain will clobber the roof with buckshot.

But still the forest is our foyer;
The moonlight beyond the pines is our stove.
The cloud babbles and dries
Everything like a new-washed apron.

If the hurricane of grief
Bursts in upon your well,
The storm will praise your housekeeping.
My darling, can you really ask for more?

The year burned up in kerosene
Like a midge flown into a lamp.
There, amid the gray-blue dawn,
It rose up sleepy, rose up wet.

It looks through the window, as through an archway.
It is old and terrifying with compassion.
The pillow is damp on its account,
It moistened it with troubled weeping.

Как утешить эту ветошь?
О, ни разу не шутивший,
Чем запущенного лета
Грусть заглохшую утишишь?

Лес навис в свинцовых пасмах,
Сед и пасмурен репейник,
Он — в слезах, а ты — прекрасна,
Вся, как день, как нетерпенье!

Что он плачет, старый олух?
Иль видал каких счастливей?
Иль подсолнечники в селах
Гаснут, — солнца, в пыль и в ливень?

How can you quiet these old rags,
You, devoid of laughter?
How will you smooth
Summer's smothered sorrow?

The forest is hung with tinsel;
The thistle is hoary with brooding.
It weeps, but you are lovely
As a day, as impatience.

What does he weep for, the old fool?
Did he never see happy people before?
Or do sunflowers fade away in villages,
As suns do in dust and cloudburst?

Распад

*Вдруг стало видимо далеко
во все концы света.*

ГОГОЛЬ

Куда часы нам затесать?
Как скоротать тебя, Распад?
Поволжьем мира, чудеса
Взялись, бушуют и не спят.

И где привык сдаваться глаз
На милость засухи степной,
Она, туманная, взвилась
Революционною копной.

По элеваторам, вдали,
В пакгаузах, очумив крысят,
Пылают балки и кули,
И кровли гаснут и росят.

У звезд немой и жаркий спор:
Куда девался Балашов?
В скольких верстах? И где Хопер?
— И воздух степи всполошен:

Он чует, он впивает дух
Солдатских бунтов и зарниц,
Он замер, обращаясь в слух,
Ложится, — слышит: обернись!

Там — гул. Ни лечь, ни прикорнуть.
По площадям летает трут.
Там ночь, шатаясь на корню,
Целует уголь поутру.

В ТО ЛЕТО ТУДА УЕЗЖАЛИ С ПАВЕЛЕЦКОГО ВОКЗАЛА.

Decay[8]

Suddenly you could see for a great distance
To the four corners of the earth.

GOGOL

To what purpose does time speed on?
Why this haste, Decay?
Like a Volga-universe miracles occur,
Blunder about, not sleeping.

And where I used to throw myself
On the grace of the barren steppe,
There, hidden in the fog,
Are revolutionary hayricks.

Among the silos in the distance
And in the warehouses the rats have gone mad.
The rafters and grain bags have burst into flame.
And the roofs cave in and turn to rot.

The stars in their silence argue hotly:
Whatever happened to Balashov?
Where is it now? Where is the River Khoper?[9]
The air across the steppe is agitated.

It feels and inhales the breath
Of soldier's riots and heat lightning,
And freezes, pricks up its ears,
Lies down, hearing: "Turn back!"

There is only the hollow echo: "No one lies down,
No taking root!" Tinder flies about the city squares.
There, night, shuddering on the stem,
Kisses the coal in the morning.

THAT SUMMER WE LEFT FROM PAVLETSKY STATION.

[85]

РОМАНОВКА

ROMANOVKA[10]

Степь

Как были те выходы в тишь хороши!
Безбрежная степь, как марина,
Вздыхает ковыль, шуршат мураши
И плавает плач комариный.

Стога с облаками построились в цепь
И гаснут, вулкан на вулкане.
Примолкла и взмокла безбрежная степь,
Колеблет, относит, толкает.

Туман отовсюду нас морем обстиг,
В волчцах волочась за чулками,
И чудно нам степью, как взморьем, брести —
Колеблет, относит, толкает.

Не стог ли в тумане? Кто поймет?
Не наш ли омет? Доходим. — Он.
— Нашли! Он самый и есть. — Омет,
Туман и степь с четырех сторон.

И млечный путь стороной ведет
На Керчь, как шлях, скотом пропылен.
Зайти за хаты, и дух займет:
Открыт, открыт с четырех сторон.

Туман снотворен, ковыль, как мед.
Ковыль всем млечным путем рассорен.
Туман разойдется и ночь обоймет
Омет и степь с четырех сторон.

Тенистая полночь стоит у пути,
На шлях навалилась звездами,
И через дорогу за тын перейти
Нельзя, не топча мирозданья.

The Steppe

How good were those walks into silence!
The boundless steppe is like a seascape.
The feather-grass sighs, the ants rustle,
The moaning of mosquitoes drifts in the sky.

The hayricks, heaped in rows with the clouds,
Fade away, volcano upon volcano.
The boundless steppe grows silent and damp;
It rocks, moves, pushes.

The mist from everywhere comes flooding like a sea,
Trailing its stockings on thistles;
Marvelously we walk the steppe, this seashore.
You shudder and drift and sway.

Are there no ricks in the mist? Who knows?
Is that our rick? Let's go!
Look! There it is, the hayrick!
Mist and steppe on every side.

The Milky Way leans toward Kerch[11]
Like a bridle path made dusty by cattle.
If you go past the peasant huts, it will take your breath
        away:
There is open space on every side!

The mist is soporific: the feather-grass is like honey.
The blades of grass tumble across the whole Milky Way.
The mist will lift and night will stretch its arms
Around the hay and steppe on every side.

A shadowy midnight stands by the wayside;
The road is overflowing with strewn stars.
You cannot go across the road to reach the fence
Without treading on the universe.

[89]

Когда еще звезды так низко росли,
И полночь в бурьян окунало,
Пылал и пугался намокший муслин,
Льнул, жался и жаждал финала?

Пусть степь нас рассудит и ночь разрешит,
Когда, когда не: — В Начале
Плыл Плач Комариный, Ползли Мураши,
Волчцы по Чулкам Торчали?

Закрой их, любимая! — Запорошит!
Вся степь, как до грехопаденья:
Вся — миром об'ята, вся — как парашют,
Вся — дыбящееся виденье!

When did the stars grow so low,
When did midnight sink deep among the weeds,
And drenched, frightened muslin flare up,
Cling closer, press down, thirsting for the finale?

Let the steppe judge and the night absolve us.
When? — if not In The Beginning
The Mosquitoes Swam In Tears, The Ants Crawled,
The Thistles Sticking Out Of Stockings.

Close them, beloved! It is powdery as snow!
The whole steppe, as before Adam's Fall —
All one embraced by the world, like a parachute,
Like a vision rising.

Душная Ночь

Накрапывало, — но не гнулись
И травы в грозовом мешке,
Лишь пыль глотала дождь в пилюлях, —
Железо в тихом порошке.

Селенье не ждало целенья,
Был мак как обморок глубок,
И рожь горела в воспаленьи
И в роже пух и бредил Бог.

В осиротелой и бессонной
Сырой, всемирной широте
С постов спасались бегством стоны,
Но вихрь, зарывшись, коротел.

За ними в бегстве слепли следом
Косые капли. У плетня
Меж мокрых веток с ветром бледным
Шел спор. Я замер. — Про меня!

Я чувствовал, он будет вечен,
Ужасный говорящий сад.
Еще я с улицы, за речью
Кустов и ставней — не замечен;
Заметят, — некуда назад:
Навек, навек заговорят.

A Sultry Night

The first rain fell, but did not bend
The grasses in the thunder's belly.
Dust merely gulped the rain down in pellets
Like iron falling in a silent powder.

The village hoped for no relief;
The poppy drowned in depths of swoon;
The rye, inflamed, was fiery red,
A hairy erysipelas. God went raving mad.

In the orphaned, sleepless, damp wastes,
All comfortless, the groans flew headlong
Along the telegraph poles.
Whirlwind settled in, then lay still.

And then the slanting, fleeing drops grew blind,
And on the fence a quarrel arose
Between the wet boughs and the pale wind —
My heart grew tense; they were talking of me!

I thought they would go on talking endlessly,
That chattering garden; and yet from the street
No one could ever see me,
While the shrubs and shutters went on talking.
If they see me, there is no turning back!
Will they go on chattering forever!

Еще Более Душный Рассвет

Все утро голубь ворковал
У вас в окне.
На желобах,
Как рукава сырых рубах,
Мертвели ветки.
Накрапывало. Налегке
Шли пыльным рынком тучи,
Тоску на рыночном лотке,
Боюсь, — мою
Баюча.
Я умолял их перестать,
Казалось, — перестанут,
Рассвет был сер, как спор в кустах,
Как говор арестантов.

Я умолял приблизить час,
Когда за окнами у вас
Нагорным ледником
Бушует умывальный таз,
И песни колотой куски,
Жар наспанной щеки, и лоб
В стекло горячее, как лед,
На подзеркальник льет.

Но высь за говором под стяг
Идущих туч
Не слышала мольбы
В запорошенной тишине,
Намокшей, как шинель,
Как пыльный отзвук молотьбы,
Как громкий спор в кустах.

An Even More Sultry Dawn

All morning a pigeon has cooed
In at your window.
In the gutters,
The boughs have withered
Like sleeves on a damp shirt.
First rain. Rather lightly
The clouds went by like a dusty market place,
Lulling
My grief, I fear
On a market hawker's tray.
I begged them to stop.
It seemed they would.
The dawn was as gray as the argument in the bushes
Or convicts' talk.

I prayed that the hour come
When at your window
The washbowl would roar
Like a mountain glacier
And pour broken sugar bits of songs
And the heat of sleep — hot cheeks and brow
Into the scorching glass,
Like ice, on the dressing table.

But the sky, for the talk
Under the banner of moving clouds,
Did not hear my request.

In the snow-dusted silence,
Drenched like an overcoat,
Like the dusty echo of threshing,
Like the loud argument in the bushes.

Я их просил —
Не мучьте!
Не спится.

Но, — моросило, и топчась
Шли пыльным рынком тучи
Как рекруты, за хутор, поутру.
Брели не час, не век,
Как пленные австрийцы,
Как тихий хрип,
Как хрип:
Испить,
Сестрица.

I begged them:
"Don't torture me!
I can't sleep."

But — a mist arose, and stamping their feet,
Clouds went by like a dusty market place,
Like recruits passing a farmhouse early in the morning.
They wandered over an hour, an age,
Like Austrian prisoners of war,
Like a low rasp,
A rasp:
"Nurse,
I'm thirsty!"

ПОПЫТКА
ДУШУ
РАЗЛУЧИТЬ

AN ATTEMPT
TO SEPARATE
THE SOUL

Мучкап

Душа — душна, и даль — табачного
Какого-то, как мысли, цвета.
У мельниц — вид села рыбачьего:
Седые сети и корветы.

Чего там ждут, томя картиною
Корыт, клешней и лишних крыльев,
Застлавши слез излишней тиною
Последний блеск на рыбьем рыле?

Ах, там и час скользит, как камешек
Заливом, мелью рикошета!
Увы, не тонет, нет, он там еще,
Табачного, как мысли цвета.

Увижу нынче ли опять ее?
До поезда ведь час. Конечно!
Но этот час об'ят апатией
Морской, предгромовой, кромешной.

Muchkap[12]

The soul is suffocating. The horizon
Is a sort of tobacco color like thought.
The mill looks like a fishing village:
Gray nets and small boats.

What are they waiting for, spoiling
The picture of troughs, claws, and mill sails,
Covering with a useless mire of tears
The last glimmer of fish snouts?

There, an hour skims like pebbles
Ricocheting in the cove, the shoal!
O, it's not sinking, it's still there,
Tobacco colored, like thought.

Shall I still see her again today?
There is still an hour to train time. Of course!
But that hour is hugged in apathy
Of sea, the moment before a thunder-clap, hell.

Мухи Мучкапской Чайной

Если бровь резьбою
Потный лоб украсила,
Значит и разбойник?
Значит за дверь, засветло?

Но в чайной, где черные вишни
Глядят из глазниц и из мисок
На веток кудрявый девичник,
Есть, есть чему изумиться!

Солнце, словно кровь с ножа,
Смысл — и стал необычаен.
Словно преступленья жар
Заливает черным чаем.

Пыльный мак паршивым пащенком
Никнет в жажде берегущей
К дню в душе его кипящему
К дикой, терпкой Божьей гуще.

Ты зовешь меня святым,
Я тебе и дик и чуден,
— А глыбастые цветы
На часах и на посуде?

Неизвестно, на какой
Из страниц земного шара
Отпечатаны рекой
Зной и тявканье овчарок,

Дуб и вывески финифть,
Не стерпевшая, и — плашмя
Кинувшаяся от ив
К прудовой курчавой яшме,

Flies of the Muchkap Tearoom

If the eyebrows decorate a sweaty brow
Like a carving, does it mean
He is a bandit? Does it mean
Get out while there is time?

But in the tearoom, where black cherries
Stare out of their eye-sockets — tureens —
At the flowery bridal shower,
There is something to stare at.

He washed the sun away like blood from a knife,
And just stood there, looking strange.
He pours out black tea
As over the passion of a crime.

The dusty poppy bends in a wary thirst
As a mangy puppy bends to the day
Boiling in his heart,
To the wild, bitter, godly dregs.

You call me holy;
I am strange and wild to you.
Are mud-clumps of flowers
On the clock and dishes?

No one knows
On which page of this earth
The day's heat and the barking of sheep dogs
Are printed like a river,

Or the oak and the enamel of sign-boards
That cannot endure
Thrown flat on their face from the willows
To the curly jasper of the pond.

Но текут и по ночам
Мухи с дюжин, пар и порций,
С крученого паныча,
С мутной книжки стихотворца.

Будто это бред с пера,
Не владеючи собою,
Брызгнул окна запирать
Саранчою по обоям.

Будто в этот час пора
Разлететься всем пружинам,
И жужжа, трясясь, спираль
Тополь бурей окружила.

Где? В каких местах? В каком
Дико мыслящемся крае?
Знаю только: в сушь и в гром,
Пред грозой, в июле, — знаю.

At night, flies flow
By dozens, pairs, portions,
From the twisted little figurine,
From the muddled book of poetry.

Just as if this were the delirium of a pen
No longer in control of itself
Spattering the windows
And the wallpaper like locusts.

Just as if this were the time for all
The springs to fly apart,
And the buzz, the shiver, the storm-spiral
Surrounded the poplar.

Where? What place was that?
In what wild corner of the world?
All I know: It was in the dryness and thunder
Just before a storm — July — That I know.

☆

Дик прием был, дик приход,
Еле ноги доволок.
Как воды набрала в рот,
Взор уперла в потолок.

Ты молчала. Ни за кем
Не рвался с такой тугой.
Если губы на замке,
Вешай с улицы другой.

Нет, не на дверь, не в пробой,
Если на сердце запрет,
Но на весь одной тобой
Немутимо белый свет.

Чтобы знал, как балки брус
По над лбом проволоку,
Что в глаза твои упрусь,
В непрорубную тоску.

Чтоб бежал с землей знакомств,
Видев издали, с пути
Гарь на солнце под замком,
Гниль на веснах взаперти.

Не вводи души в обман,
Оглуши, завесь, забей.
Пропитала, как туман,
Груду белых отрубей.

Если душным полднем желт
Мышью пахнущий овин,
Обличи, скажи, что лжет
Лжесвидетельство любви.

☆

The reception was wild; the entrance, wild.
My feet had barely strength to move.
How your mouth watered;
You trained your glances on the ceiling.

You were silent. I never desired anyone
As I did you.
If your lips were locked in silence,
Then hang another on the door.

No, not from the door or the keyhole,
If it is locked inside the heart,
But inside the whole world,
So unperturbed for you.

So that I understand
I will drag a crossbeam over my brow—
Understand how to search in your eyes
For your inconsolable grief.

So that I would flee with my world of acquaintances,
Seeing from afar how along the road
The scorching of the sun was under lock and key
And all the rot of the spring weather was locked up.

Do not let the soul go astray,
Do not deaden, veil, or pile-drive it.
Like the fog, it has already swamped
The heaps of white chaff.

If the midday barn that smells of mice
Is yellow with the heat of day,
Accuse and say: Love's false witness
Is the one that tells lies.

☆

Попытка душу разлучить
С тобой, как жалоба смычка,
Еще мучительно звучит
В названьях Ржакса и Мучкап

Я их, как будто это ты,
Как будто это ты сама,
Люблю всей силою тщеты
До помрачения ума.

Как ночь, уставшую сиять,
Как то, что в астме — кисея,
Как то, что даже антресоль
При виде плеч твоих трясло.

Чей шопот реял на брезгу?
О, мой ли? — нет, душою — твой,
Он улетучивался с губ
Воздушней капли спиртовой.

Как в неге прояснялась мысль!
Безукоризненно. Как стон.
Как пеной, в полночь, с трех сторон
Внезапно озаренный мыс.

☆

The attempt to separate my soul from yours
Is like the sobbing of a violin bow.
I again painfully recall
The names of Rzhaksa[13] and Muchkap.

I love them, as if they were you;
You, yourself;
I love them with all the power of futility
Even to the point of obscuring thought.

Like night grown tired of shining,
Like muslin in asthma,
Even the balcony trembled
At the sight of your shoulders.

Whose whisper fluttered along so timidly?
Was it mine? No, yours, your soul's.
It evaporated on your lips,
More volatile than drops of alcohol.

A serious thought appeared in the midst of languor
Blameless. Like a groan.
Like foam at midnight, like a headland
Suddenly lit from three sides.

ВОЗВРАЩЕНИЕ

THE RETURN

☆

Как усыпительна жизнь!
Как откровенья бессонны!
Можно ль тоску размозжить
Об мостовые кессоны?

Где с железа ночь согнал
Каплей копленый сигнал,
И колеблет всхлипы звезд
В апокалипсисе мост,
Переплет, цепной обвал
Балок, ребер, рельс и шпал,
Где шатаясь подают
Руки, падают, поют,
Из об'ятий, и — опять,
Не устанут повторять, —
Где внезапно зонд вонзил
В лица вспыхнувший бензин
И остался как загар,
На тупых концах сигар —

Это огненный тюльпан,
Полевой огонь бегоний
Жадно нюхает толпа,
Заслонив ладонью.

И сгорают, как в стыде
Пыльники, нежнее лент,
Каждый пятый — инженер
И студент — (интеллигенты).

Я с ними незнаком.
Я послан Богом мучить
Себя, родных и тех,
Которых мучить грех.

How sleepy life is,
And how sleepless life's revelations!
Can one smash the skull of yearning
On the foundations of bridges?

The railroad signal, swollen like a dewdrop,
Derailed the night;
Where the bridge shivers
In an apocalypse of wailing stars,
And timbers and ribs and rails and railroad ties
Are rolled together in an involved avalanche;
Where the rocking human hands arise,
Fall, and burst into song.
And from embraces there comes — again
Untiring, and the words repeat.
Where suddenly the dip-stick
Stuck flaring gasoline in their faces
And there remained this sunburn,
Like the tips of burned-out cigars —

This, the flame-red tulip,
The field artillery of begonias,
The masses greedily inhale,
Shielding their eyes with their hands.
And the engineer,
The student, a fifth of the nation (intellectuals)
Are burned as in shame
By pistils, more delicate than ribbons.

I have no knowledge of these people.
I was sent by God to torment
Myself, my relatives, and those
Who are tormented by sin.

Под Киевом — пески
И выплеснутый чай,
Присохший к жарким лбам,
Пылающим по классам.
Под Киевом, в числе
Песков, как кипяток,
Как смытый пресный след
Компресса, как отек —

Пыхтенье, сажу, жар
Не соснам разжижать.
Гроза торчит в бору
Как всоженный топор.
Но где он, дроворуб?
До коих пор? Какой
Тропой итти в депо?

Сажают пассажиров,
Дают звонок, свистят,
Чтоб копоть послужила
Пустыней миг спустя.

Базары, озаренья
Ночных эспри и мглы,
А днем, в сухой спирее
Вопль полдня и пилы.

Идешь, и с запасных
Доносится, как всхнык,
И начали стираться
Клохтанья и матрацы.

Я с ними незнаком.
Я послан Богом мучить
Себя, родных и тех,
Которых мучить грех.

Near Kiev, the sands
And the slopped tea
Dried out on the warm brows,
Blazing according to the classes.
Near Kiev, according to the number of sands,
Like the boiling of water,
Or the clean, washed traces of a compress,
Or an inflammation —

Puffing, soot, heat
Are not for pine trees to dilute.
The thunderstorm sticks in the pine wood
Like a protruding ax.
But where is the woodsman?
And how long will this go on?
Where is the path to the trainyard?

The passengers are seated,
The whistle blows, the bell rings,
And clouds of soot produce a wilderness
A moment later.

Bazaars, nightlong illuminations,
Of feathered hats, shadows,
And during the day, in the dry dune roses,
The howl of noonday and a handsaw.

You walk along
And there seems to be someone sobbing
In the sheds. The clack of tongue
And mattresses are being hung out to air.

I have no knowledge of these people.
I was sent by God to torment
Myself, my relatives, and those
Who are tormented by sin.

«Мой сорт», кефир, менадо,
— Чтоб разрыдаться, мне
Совсем немного надо,
Довольно мух в окне.

Охлынет поле зренья,
С салфетки набежит,
От поросенка в хрене,
Как с полусонной ржи.

Чтоб разрыдаться, мне
По край, чтоб из редакций
Тянуло табачком
И падал жар ничком.

Чтоб щелкали с кольца
Клесты по канцеляриям
И тучи в огурцах
С отчаянья стрелялись.

Чтоб полдень осязал
Сквозь сон: в обед трясутся
По звону квизисан
Столы в пустых присутствиях.

И на лоб по жаре
Сочились сквозь малинник,
Где — блеск оранжерей,
Где — белый корпус клиники.

Я с ними незнаком.
Я послан Богом мучить
Себя, родных и тех,
Которых мучить грех.

"My Brand," kefir, Menado,[14]
It does not take much to make me cry:
A fly on the windowpane will do.

It will overflow the field of vision,
It will roll down from the napkin,
From the suckling pig in the horseradish,
And from the half-sleeping rye.

To have a good cry,
All I need is the odor of tobacco
From the editor's room, or the heat
Falling headlong on the street;

Or the click of a crossbill's beak
In the offices,
Or clouds opening fire
Out of boredom on cucumbers;

Or noon appearing through a dream,
Or tables at empty sittings
Shaking at dinnertime
With the sound of cafés;

Or the trickle from a raspberry bush
In the heat on my brow,
There, where the hothouse glitters,
There, where the white form of the clinic lies.

I have no knowledge of these people.
I was sent by God to torment
Myself, my relatives, and those
Who are tormented by sin.

Возможно ль? Этот полдень
Сейчас, южней губернией,
Не сир, не бос, не голоден,
Блаженствует, соперник?

Вот этот, душный, лишний,
Вокзальный вор, валандала
Следит с соседних вишен
За вышиваньем ангела?

Синеет морем точек,
И низясь, тень без косточек
Бросает, горсть за горстью
Измученной сорочке?

Возможно ль? Те вот ивы —
Их гонят с рельс шлагбаумами —
Бегут в об'ятья дива,
Обращены на взбалмошность?

Перенесутся за ночь,
С крыльца вдохнут эссенции
И бросятся хозяйничать
Порывом полотенец?

Увидят тень орешника
На каменном фундаменте?
Узнают день, сгоревший
С восхода на свиданьи?

Зачем тоску упрямить
Перебирая мелочи?
Нам изменяет память
И гонит с рельсов стрелочник.

Is it possible? This noon,
Now more southern than the provinces,
Is not dry, nor barefoot, nor hungry,
And shall the competitor rejoice?

Look! Is that breathless, useless
Trainyard thief, that loiterer,
Looking for angel embroideries
In his neighbor's cherries?

Is he turning blue like a sea of asterisks
And, coming down, does he hurl
Handful after handful of seedless,
Marrowless shadows at a martyred nightgown?

Is it possible? Those willows, there,
Are they driven from the rails by barricades?
Do they run, turned giddy,
To the embrace of a miracle?

Will they last the night?
Will essences breathe life from the wings?
And will they give up trying to make do
With the gusts of hand towels?

Will people see the hazel-bush shadow
On the stone foundation?
Will they recognize the day,
Burned from sunrise to the rendezvous?

Why persist in grief,
Sorting out trivialities?
Our memories fail us,
And the switchman is shunting us off the tracks.

У Себя Дома

Жар на семи холмах,
Голуби в тлелом сенце.
С солнца спадает чалма:
Время менять полотенце
(— Мякнет на днище ведра. —)
И намотать на купол.

В городе — говор мембран,
Шарканье клумб и кукол.
Надо гардину зашить:
— Ходит, шагает массоном.
Как усыпительно — жить!
Как целоваться — бессонно!

Грязный, гремучий, — в постель
Падает город с дороги.
Нынче за долгую степь
Веет впервые здоровьем.
Черных имен духоты
Не исчерпать.
Звезды, плацкарты, мосты, —
— Спать!

С ПАВЕЛЕЦКОГО ЖЕ УЕЗЖАЛИ И В ТУ ОСЕНЬ.

At Home

Heat hangs on seven hills;[15]
Doves on the mildewed hay;
A turban slips from the sun;
It is time to change the towel
(Soaking at the bottom of the pail)
And wind it round the dome.

In the town they talk of vocal chords,
Pacing gardens and of dolls.
A curtain will have to be sewn up.
And somebody is walking around like a Mason.
How narcotic to be alive!
Kissing is an insomnia!

All soiled and groaning,
The city stumbles in from the street to bed.
Now from the broad steppe
Come the first healthy breezes.
There is no end to the profanities
For this oppressive heat.
Stars, posters, and bridges —
All lead to sleep!

WE LEFT THAT AUTUMN BY WAY OF PAVLETSKY STATION.

ЕЛЕНЕ

TO HELEN

Елене

Я и непечатным
Словом не побрезговал бы,
Да на ком искать нам?
Не на ком и не с кого нам.

Разве просит арум
У болота милостыни?
Ночи дышут даром
Тропиками гнилостными.

Будешь, — думал, чаял,
Ты с того утра виднеться,
Век в душе качаясь
Лилиею, праведница!

Луг дружил с замашкой
Фауста что ли, Гамлета ли,
— Обегал ромашкой,
Стебли по ногам летали.

Или еле-еле,
Как сквозь сон овеивая
Жемчуг ожерелья
На плече Офелиином.

Ночью бредил хутор:
Спать мешали перистые
Тучи. Дождик кутал
Ниву тихой переступью

Осторожных капель.
Юность в счастьи плавала, как
В тихом детском храпе
Наспанная наволока.

To Helen

I would not take umbrage
Over an unprinted word.
Where can one search?
Nowhere, no one.

Does the jack-in-the-pulpit
Beg alms of the marshes?
In vain do the nights reek
Of decaying pathways.

You will be (I thought, felt,
That from that morning on I would see you)
In the heart a century
Like a lily, still virtuous one!

The meadow made Faust, yes,
Even Hamlet, friend to habit;
He stamped on the camomile;
Stalks flew at his feet;

Or, barely breathing,
As in a dream,
Strands of pearls
On Ophelia's shoulders.

At night the cottage went mad.
Plumes of clouds prevented sleep.
With a quiet tread,
The cautious rainfall hid the cornfield.

Youth swam in joy,
Like a pillowcase
Under the quiet breathing
Of a sleeping child.

Думал, — Трои б век ей,
Горьких губ изгиб целуя:
Были дивны веки
Царственные, гипсовые.

Милый, мертвый фартук
И висок пульсирующий,
Спи, царица Спарты,
Рано еще, сыро еще.

Горе не на шутку
Разыгралось, навеселе,
Одному с ним жутко
Сбесится, — управиться ли?

Плачь, шепнуло. Гложет?
Жжет? — Такую ж на щеку ей! —
Пусть судьба положит,
Матерью ли, мачехой ли.

I thought Troy had had its day
In the twisted kisses of her bitter lips.
Ah, those were centuries of marvels,
Imperial, plaster-of-Paris times!

Dear, dead apron
And pulsating temple.
Sleep, Empress of Sparta,
It is still early, still dewy.

Drunk and in its cups, sorrow
Has not played the fool for a joke.
To be alone with him is terrifying.
If he goes mad, can you manage?

Cry, it whispered. Does it hurt?
Does it sting? On her cheeks, so!
Let fate decide: Was she
A mother or a foster mother!

Как У Них

Лицо лазури пышет над лицом
Недышущей любимицы реки.
Подымется, шелохнется ли сом, —
— Оглушены. Не слышут. Далеки́.

Очам в снопах, как кровлям, тяжело.
Как угли блещут оба очага.
Лицо лазури пышет над челом
Недышущей подруги в бочагах,
Недышущей питомицы осок.

То ветер смех люцерны вдоль высот,
Как поцелуй воздушный пронесет,
То княженикой с топи угощен,
Ползет и губы пачкает хвощем
И треплет речку веткой по щеке,
То киснет и хмелеет в тростнике.

У окуня ли екнут плавники, —
Бездонный день — огромен и пунцов,
Поднос Шелони — черен и свинцов,
Не свесть концов и не поднять руки...

Лицо лазури пышет над лицом
Недышущей любимицы реки.

But They

A face of azure gleams above the face
Of his not-breathing and beloved river.
A catfish stirs and starts.
They are deaf; hear nothing; are far off.

The eyes in the sheaves are as heavy as roofs,
Like coals, with both hearths glowing.
A face of azure gleams above the brow
Of his not-breathing lady of the deep,
Of his not-breathing nurseling of the marsh grass.

The wind will carry the laughter of alfalfa
Along the ridges, like blowing kisses,
And regaling itself with the marshland's berries,
It creeps along, smears its lips with the water fern,
And flutters a branch on the river's cheek,
Or sours and ferments among the reeds.

Do the perch's fins begin to throb —
The depthless day is huge and crimson;
The surface of the Shelon,[16] black and leaden colored.
No ends to make meet and no hands to raise . . .

A face of azure gleams above the face
Of his not-breathing and beloved river.

Лето

Тянулось в жажде к хоботкам
И бабочкам и пятнам,
Обоим память оботкав
Медовым, майным, мятным.

Не ход часов, но звон цепов
С восхода до захода
Вонзался в воздух сном шипов,
Заворожив погоду.

Бывало — нагулявшись всласть,
Закат сдавал цикадам
И звездам и деревьям власть
Над кухнею и садом.

Не тени, — балки месяц клал,
А то бывал в отлучке,
И тихо, тихо ночь текла
Трусцой, от тучки к тучке.

Скорей со сна, чем с крыш: скорей
Забывчивый, чем робкий —
Топтался дождик у дверей
И пахло винной пробкой.

Так пахла пыль. Так пах бурьян.
И если разобраться,
Так пахли прописи дворян
О равенстве и братстве.

Вводили земство в волостях;
С другими — вы, не так ли?
Дни висли, в кислице блестя;
И винной пробкой пахли.

Summer

Mosquito-beak and blur of butterfly
Distend in thirst and leave the meady
Minty, May mementos
All over the walls.

No tread of time, only the lash of flails,
From sunrise to sunset,
Is driven into the air, like a dream
Of thorns bewitching weather.

There was a time you could stroll at your pleasure
And sunset used to grant to crickets,
To trees and stars the power to rule
The kitchen and the kitchen garden.

Not shadows, but the moon
Would gild ravines, then disappear,
And quietly, quietly night oozed away
Like a coward, from cloud to cloud.

More from a dream than from roofs,
And more carelessly than timidly,
The raindrops seemed to kick at doors
And it smelled outdoors like a wine cork.

That is how dust used to smell; thus, the shrubby weeds;
And if you really analyze the thing,
That is how aristocratic maxims smelled
On the subject of equality and fraternity.

The Zemstvo[17] was opened in country areas;
You were with the rest, was it not so?
The days hung bright in the wood sorrel,
And it smelled outdoors like a wine cork.

Гроза, Моментальная Навек

А затем прощалось лето
С полустанком. Снявши шапку
Сто слепящих фотографий
Ночью снял на память гром.

Меркла кисть сирени. В это
Время он, нарвав охапку
Молний, с поля ими трафил
Озарить управский дом.

И когда по кровле зданья
Разлилась волна злорадства,
И как уголь по рисунку,
Грянул ливень всем плетнем,

Стал мигать обвал сознанья:
Вот, казалось, озарятся
Даже те углы рассудка,
Где теперь светло, как днем!

A Momentary Thunderstorm Forever

Afterward Summer said farewell
To the little village. Doffing his cap
Thunder snapped a hundred blinding
Photographs at night for keepsakes.

Clumps of lilacs faded. Then
With an armful of lightning,
It hurled them straight from the meadow
To illuminate an official's house.

And when the wave of malice poured
Along the building's roof
And the downpour rattled on the fences
Like charcoal on a drawing pad,

Then an avalanche of consciousness.
Well, it seems that even
Those corners of reason, now light as day,
Will get illumination, too.

ПОСЛЕСЛОВЬЕ

EPILOGUE

☆

Любимая — жуть! Когда любит поэт,
Влюбляется Бог неприкаянный.
И хаос опять выползает на свет,
Как во времена ископаемых.

Глаза ему тонны туманов слезят.
Он застлан. Он кажется мамонтом.
Он вышел из моды. Он знает — нельзя:
Прошли времена, и — безграмотно.

Он видит, как свадьбы справляют вокруг,
Как спаивают, просыпаются,
Как общелягушечью эту икру
Зовут, обрядив ее, — паюсной.

Как жизнь, как жемчужную шутку Ватто
Умеют обнять табакеркою,
И мстят ему, может быть, только за то,
Что там, где кривят и коверкают,

Где лжет и кадит, ухмыляясь, комфорт,
И трутнями трутся и ползают,
Он вашу сестру, как вакханку с амфор,
Подымет с земли и использует.

И таянье Андов вольет в поцелуй,
И утро в степи, под владычеством
Пылящихся звезд, когда ночь по селу
Белеющим блеяньем тычется.

И всем, чем дышалось оврагам века,
Всей тьмой ботанической ризницы
Пахнет по тифозной тоске тюфяка,
И хаосом зарослей брызнется.

☆

Beloved — terror! When a poet loves,
The unrepentant god is infatuated,
And chaos again crawls out into the light
In some prehistoric age of fossils.

His eyes weep with tons of clouds.
He is overcast. He is like a mammoth.
He is out of fashion. He knows it is wrong —
Old fashioned! It is positively boorish!

He sees weddings everywhere,
How they get drunk and sleep it off.
He sees you can call common frog spawn
Pressed caviar as long as you adorn it;

Or how people squeeze life into a cigarette case
Like Watteau's joke about pearls, and
Revenge themselves on him, perhaps only because
There, where they distend, they distort life,

Where smirking comfort tells lies, lops pieces off,
And they rub shoulders with loafers and crawl —
Because there he lifts your sister from the ground
Like a drunken Bacchante on a Greek vase and uses her.

And the thawing of the Andes flows into a kiss,
And morning onto the steppes under the dominion
Of flaming stars, and in the village
The night nuzzles with a white bleating.

And what the ravines smelled of for ages,
All the darkness of that botanical sacristy,
Comes the odor of the typhoid grief of the mattress,
And it rains with a chaos of weeds.

☆

Мой друг, ты спросишь, кто велит,
Чтоб жглась юродивого речь?

Давай ронять слова,
Как сад — янтарь и цедру,
Рассеянно и щедро,
Едва, едва, едва.

Не надо толковать,
Зачем так церемонно
Мареной и лимоном
Обрызнута листва.

Кто иглы заслезил
И хлынул через жерди
На ноты, к этажерке
Сквозь шлюзы жалюзи,

Кто коврик за дверьми
Рябиной иссурьмил,
Рядном сквозных, красивых,
Трепещущих курсивов.

Ты спросишь, кто велит,
Чтоб август был велик,
Кому ничто не мелко,
Кто погружен в отделку

Кленового листа
И с дней экклезиаста
Не покидал поста
За теской алебастра?

Ты спросишь, кто велит
Чтоб губы астр и далий
Сентябрьские страдали?

☆

My friend, you ask by whose command
The words of God's fool are burned? . . .[18]

Lets the words fall
Like a garden — amber and lemon peel,
Bountifully seeded and scattered,
Scarcely, scarcely, scarcely.

There is no need to explain
Why the leaves are sprinkled
With gardenia and lemon,
With pomp and ceremony.

Who set the thorns to tears,
Gushed through the fences
Into music, to the bookcase,
Through the sluice of the jalousies?

Who colored the doormat
Like a mountain ash
With a design transparent and beautiful
Of trembling italics.

You ask by whose command
August should be great.
To whom a nothing is not trivial;
Who is enmeshed in the minutia
Of maple leaves,
And who, since the days of Ecclesiastes,
Never left his post
At the hewing of alabaster?

You ask by whose command
The lips of September asters
And dahlias are made to suffer.

[139]

Чтоб мелкий лист ракит
С седых кариатид
Слетал на сырость плит
Осенних госпиталей?
Ты спросишь, кто велит?
— Всесильный Бог деталей,
Всесильный Бог любви,
Ягайлов и Ядвиг.

Не знаю, решена ль
Загадка зги загробной,
Но жизнь, — как тишина
Осенняя — подробна.

Or the fragile willow leaf
Falls from the gray caryatids
Onto the damp gravestones
Of autumn hospitals?
You ask: By whose command?
The omnipotent god of details;
The omnipotent god of love,
Of Yagailos and Yadrigas.[19]

I do not know whether the riddle
Of the void beyond the grave has been solved.
But life is not unlike
An autumn calm.

Имелось

Засим, имелся сеновал
И пахнул винной пробкой
С тех дней, что август миновал
И не пололи тропки.

В траве, на кислице, меж бус
Брилльянты, хмурясь, висли,
По захладелости на вкус
Напоминая рислинг.

Сентябрь составлял статью
В извощичьем хозяйстве,
Летал, носил и по чутью
Предупреждал ненастье.

То, застя двор, водой с винцом
Желтил песок и лужи,
То с неба спрынцевал свинцом
Оконниц полукружья.

То золотил их, залетев
С куста за хлев, к крестьянам,
То к нашему стеклу, с дерев
Пожаром листьев прянув.

Есть марки счастья. Есть слова
Vin gai, vin triste, — но верь мне,
Что кислица — травой трава,
А рислинг — пыльный термин.

Имелась ночь. Имелось губ
Дрожание. На веках висли
Брилльянты, хмурясь. Дождь в мозгу
Шумел, не отдаваясь мыслью.

Was

Afterward there was the hayloft,
It smelled like a wine cork
Ever since August passed away
And they stopped weeding the paths.

In the grass, in the sorrel,
The sullen diamonds hung between the beads;
And from their coolness
You would judge that they tasted of Riesling.

September wrote an article
On the economics of cab drivers,
Flew, floated, and from its feel
Anticipated the winter weather.

Now the stagnant courtyard,
Like water with wine, yellowed the sand and puddles;
Now it spattered hot lead from the sky
On half-rounded dormer windows.

It turned them gold, flying
From bushes to cattle sheds and peasants,
Now leaping at our windowpane
In a raging fire of leaves.

There are brands of joy. There is a phrase:
Vin gai, vin triste. But believe me
The wood is wood and grass is grass,
And Riesling is a dusty word.

There was a night. There was the trembling
Of lips. Diamonds hung on eyelids,
Sullen droplets. Rain roared in the brain,
And there was no surrendering to thought.

Казалось, не люблю, — молюсь
И не целую, — мимо
Не век, не час плывет моллюск,
Свеченьем счастья тмимый.

Как музыка: — века в слезах,
А песнь не смеет плакать,
Тряслась, не прорываясь в ах! —
Коралловая мякоть.

It seems I do not love . . . I pray
But do not kiss. Frail as the glint
Of joy, a mollusk swims by
Not for a century, not even for an hour.

Like music: weeping for centuries; but the song
Dares not shed a tear.
She quivers without uttering an "Ah" —

☆

Любить, — итти, — не смолкнул гром,
Топтать тоску, не знать ботинок,
Пугать ежей, платить добром
За зло брусники с паутиной.

Пить с веток, бьющих по лицу,
Лазурь с отскоку полосуя:
«Так это эхо!» — и к концу
С дороги сбиться в поцелуях.

Как с маршем, бресть с репьем на всем.
К закату знать, что солнце старше
Тех звезд и тех телег с овсом,
Той Маргариты и корчмарши.

Терять язык, абонемент
На бурю слез в глазах валькирий
И в жар всем небом онемев,
Топить мачтовый лес в эфире.

Разлегшись, сгресть, в шипах, клочьми
Событья лет, как шишки ели:
Шоссе; сошествие Корчмы;
Светало; зябли; рыбу ели.

И раз свалясь, запеть: «Седой,
Я шел и пал без сил. Когда-то
Давился город лебедой,
Купавшейся в слезах солдаток.

В тени безлунных длинных риг,
В огнях баклаг и бакалеен,
Наверное и он — старик

☆

To love — to walk — the thunder still rumbles;
To trample yearning, not to know one's shoes,
To frighten hedgehogs, to repay evil
With good, cranberries with cobwebs.

To drink off branches that whip across the face
And slash the sky leaping back:
"Yes, there is the echo!" — And finally,
To lose one's way in kissing.

As on the march to make one's way with turnips
        everywhere.
To know by sunset that the sun is older
Than those stars and those wagons laden with oats,
Than that Margareta and the innkeepers.

To lose your tongue like a season ticket
To a storm of tears in the eyes of the Valkyries,
And, numb as the sky in the heat,
To drown a forest of masts in the ether.

Stretched out, to rake up the past like pine cones,
To tatters in the thorns: A highway.
Stopping off at the inn. Dawn.
You were frozen. You ate fish.

All of a sudden, you made a fool of yourself
And sang: "Old and broken, I walked and fell without
        strength.
Once, the town was choked with a pigweed
That bathed in the tears of soldiers' wives.

In the shadow of the shadow of the moonless threshing
        barn,
In the flame of flagons and foodstuffs,
Indeed, even he, the old man,

И тоже следом околеет».

———

Так пел я, пел, и умирал,
И умирал, и возвращался
К ее рукам, как бумеранг,
И, — сколько помнится — прощался.

Will croak pretty soon!"

———

That is what I sang, I sang and then died,
Died and returned to her arms,
Like a boomerang, and (as far
As I can recall) I said farewell.

Послесловье

Нет, не я вам печаль причинил.
Я не стоил забвения родины.
Это солнце горело на каплях чернил,
Как в кистях запыленной смородины,

И в крови моих мыслей и писем
Завелась кошениль.
Этот пурпур червца от меня не зависел.
Нет, не я вам печаль причинил.

Это вечер из пыли лепился, и пышучи,
Целовал вас, задохнувшись в охре, пыльцой.
Это тени вам щупали пульс. Это, вышедши
За плетень, вы полям подставляли лицо
И пылали, плывя по олифе калиток,
Полумраком, золою и маком залитых.

Это — круглое лето, горев в ярлыках
По прудам, как багаж солнопеком заляпанных,
Сургучем опечатало грудь бурлака
И сожгло ваши платья и шляпы.

Это ваши ресницы слипались от яркости
Это диск одичалый, рога истесав
Об ограды, бодаясь, крушил палисад.
Это — запад, карбункулом вам в волоса
Залетев и гудя, угасал в полчаса,
Осыпая багрянец с малины и бархатцев,
Нет, не я, это — вы, это ваша краса.

Epilogue

No, it was not I who caused you grief.
I did not deserve oblivion from my native land.
What did it was the sun aflame on ink drops
As on clusters of dusty currants.

In the blood of my thoughts and writing
Cochineal was running.
This red insect dye did not depend on me.
No, it was not I who caused you grief.

It was the evening modeled by the dust.
It kissed you, breathing the red ochre pollen.
It was the shadows feeling your pulse.
It was you swinging the gate on its oiled hinge,
And putting your face to the meadows
That burned with dusk, dust, and poppies.

It was the whole summer sorrowing in pools
Like labels on baggage torn in the tropics
That stamped the breast of the Volga bargeman with
      sealing wax
And set your hats and frocks on fire.

It was your eyelashes sticking together in the brightness.
It was the savage sunlight cutting its horns on the wall,
Goring them, knocking down the fences.
It was the West lighting in your hair like a jewel,
Humming, expiring within the hour, spreading among the
      purple
Of raspberries and African marigolds.
No, it was not I; it was you, your beauty.

КОНЕЦ

THE END

✩

Наяву ли все? Время ли разгуливать?
Лучше вечно спать, спать, спать, спать,
И не видеть снов.

Снова — улица. Снова — полог тюлевый.
Снова, что ни ночь, — степь, стог, стон
И теперь и впредь.

Листьям в августе, с астмой в каждом атоме
Снится тишь и темь. Вдруг бег пса
Пробуждает сад.

Ждет, улягутся. Вдруг — гигант из затеми,
И другой. Шаги. «Тут есть болт».
Свист и зов: тубо!

Он буквально ведь обливал, обваливал
Нашим шагом шлях! Он и тын
Истязал тобой.

Осень. Изжелта сизый бисер нижется.
Ах, как и тебе, прель, мне смерть
Как приелось жить!

О, не во-время ночь кадит маневрами
Паровозов; — в дождь каждый лист
Рвется в степь, как те.

Окна сцены мне делают. Бесцельно ведь!
Рвется с петель дверь, целовав
Лед ее локтей.

☆

Is anything real? Is it time to go
For a stroll? Better to sleep forever, sleep, sleep, sleep,
And not to dream dreams.

Again, the street. Again, the canopy of satin.
Again, what is not night, steppe, hayrick, groan,
Now and in the future.

Silence and shadows are the dreams of leaves in August
With asthma in every atom. Suddenly the running of a dog
Arouses the garden.

It waits; they will settle down. All of a sudden, a giant out
        of the darkness before the dawn!
Another one. Steps. "Here's the latch."
A whistle and a shout: "Here!"

He literally poured over, heaped
The road with our steps! He tortured the fence
With you.

Autumn. The yellow-blue pearl is threaded.
How tired you are of decay,
And I of living!

O, the night does not flatter in time
With its engine maneuvers; in the rain every leaf longs for
The steppe like the others.

My windows are making a scene. In vain, indeed!
The door will burst from its hinge after kissing
The ice of her elbows.

Познакомь меня с кем-нибудь из вскормленных,
Как они, страдой южных нив,
Пустырей и ржи.

Но с оскоминой, но с оцепененьем, с комьями
В горле, но с тоской стольких слов
Устаешь дружить!

Acquaint me with someone who has been breast-fed
Like people at harvest-time in southern fields,
Fallow lands and rye.

But with gritting of teeth, with numbness, lumps in the
      throat,
But with the sorrow of so many words,
You get tired of being friendly.

TRANSLATOR'S NOTE

I have based this translation on the original Russian text which appeared in 1922. Subsequent editions, appearing in various collections published in Pasternak's lifetime, show a number of emendations, rejections, and interpolations which are rarely of any great significance. Most of these are indicated in the collection of Pasternak's poetry (in Russian) published by the University of Michigan (1961) and in the recent collection published in Moscow (1965) with an introduction by Andrey Sinyavsky, which purports to be a final text. In these works the curious reader will find a concise record of the variant texts, so far as they are known. I have not given the variants here, and the text printed on the left-hand pages faithfully follows the original edition.

Just as I was struck by the lack of any great significance in the changes made by Pasternak over the years, so I was impressed as I proceeded with the translation with the total poetic unity of the original edition. Pasternak's later revisions were perhaps due to a change in attitude toward the work of his youth, and perhaps also to the natural meddlesomeness which authors sometimes display regarding their own work. It would be unfair to charge Pasternak with not being able to let well enough alone. Whatever his reasons for altering certain poems, I have tried to preserve the original unity and mood of this great lyric cycle, as it came fresh from his pen. These poems may be compared to Housman's *A Shropshire Lad,* Whitman's *Leaves of Grass,* and Goethe's *Westoestliche Divan,* song cycles which were conceived under a single lyrical impulse and executed in a short span of time. For such poems there can be no going back, no room for change once the last words are written and separated from their creator. When the poems are completed, the experiences are beyond recall. All is finality. To this aspect of *Sister My Life* I have attempted to remain loyal.

The recent Soviet edition of Pasternak's poetry came as a welcome surprise after the decades of suppression of his work. I have relied heavily on it for hints as to the meaning of a few cruxes that were hitherto unintelligible. Many of the notes are derived from the Soviet edition. Pasternak's own notes appear in small capitals.

In translating, I have avoided almost all rhyme. Russian is

much richer in rhymes than English. Moreover, Pasternak is not only a difficult poet in terms of vocabulary and syntax, but he uses in addition to rhyme abundant internal rhymes, alliteration, assonance, and myriad other poetic devices. On the authority of Robert Frost, who frequently said that poetry was that which was lost in translation, I decided early in my work that if something must be lost in my translation — and doubtless there is some lack — then it would be the rhyme.

By omitting the rhyme I was able to concentrate on the meaning and the images which Pasternak heaps to overflowing, and to attempt to capture as much of the inner rhyme and assonance as I could without straining the meaning. And sometimes even this music had to go by the board in order to remain true to the meaning.

Pasternak is a devil of a poet. Not only does he frequently short-circuit the norms of Russian grammar and syntax to his own poetic ends, but sometimes he even conjures up words and grammatical forms that are to be found in no vocabulary or grammar of the language. Examples of this are scattered throughout the Russian text. In addition to this aspect of his art, Pasternak with his love of music frequently puts words together for no other reason than their music. In this way he tends to strain the meaning, although the beautiful sounds he produces are almost always excuse enough. For the reader who commands Russian, good examples of these musical effects may be found in "About These Poems" (especially lines 2, 9, 13, 17–20), "A Girl," and "Rain." In this ingenious intermingling of music and meaning Pasternak remains true to the lyrical form he has chosen.

Sister My Life is a lyric cycle that celebrates Pasternak's love affair with an unknown woman in the summer of 1917. Nothing is known about the love affair except what the poet chose to reveal in his poetry. His passion is commemorated in sonorous, evocative music, and sometimes we have the impression that words and phrases may possess intimate and personal meanings that defy translation. The love affair appears to have been brief and stormy. In poem after poem we encounter whirlwinds, snowstorms, lightning and thunder, underscoring the poet's mood. Finally in the last poems we meet images of decay and death. Autumn comes, and the musty odor of wine. As the receding passion receives its ironic bon voyage, the bottle is uncorked, the toast is drunk, farewells are said, and the affair is over. Then the last poem is written, and the book is closed.

One day many years ago, Professor E. J. Simmons of the Slavic Department of Columbia University suggested in class that someone ought to translate Pasternak's *Sister My Life,* for he felt that this was the poet's greatest work.

Rosalind Zoglin has well earned my thanks for her care in so many matters that concern this book. To Eugenie Korvin-Kroukovsky and Pierre Sidamon-Eristoff, my gratitude for their sage advice.

Until now this book has been known in English as *My Sister Life*. I have adopted *Sister My Life* in the belief that it is the more accurate title. Hopefully this closer translation will compensate for the bibliographical confusion.

NOTES

1. "The Demon." Lermontov's autobiographical and romantic poem about the Caucasus.
2. Tamara. Heroine of "The Demon."
3. Dáryal Pass. A hazardous gorge in the Caucasus.
4. Balashov. A city in the Saratov district.
5. Kerensky. Prime Minister of the short-lived Provisional Government between the fall of the Tsarist regime and the October 1917 Revolution.
6. Tivoli. According to the 1965 Russian edition, an outdoor restaurant in Moscow is referred to. But possibly either the famous estate near Rome or the equally famous gardens in Copenhagen are also meant.
7. Sparrow Hills. A very hilly, picturesque area outside Moscow.
8. Raspad. A train stop. Here Pasternak is obviously making a pun, which is untranslatable, on the name of the railroad station Raspad, which means decay.
9. River Khoper. In the Saratov district.
10. Romanovka. A town in the Saratov district.
11. Kerch. A city in southern Russia.
12. Muchkap. A small town near Balashov.
13. Rzhaksa. A town near Balashov.
14. My Brand. A brand of cigarettes; kefir. A Caucasian drink made from fermented milk; Menado. A brand of coffee.
15. Seven hills. Moscow, like Rome and Constantinople, is situated on seven hills.
16. Shelon. A river in the Pskov district.
17. Zemstvo. The pre-revolutionary elective provincial legislative body established in 1864.
18. *My friend, you ask by whose command,* etc. A quotation from Pasternak's own poem, "Balashov," earlier in the book, p. 35.
19. Yagailov and Yadviga. The 1965 Russian edition tells us that these two persons were a Lithuanian prince and a Polish queen, respectively, whose marriage in ancient times ushered in the first Polish-Lithuanian union, 1386 A.D.

Указатель
по
Первой Строчке

Index
to
First Lines

ABOUT THE AUTHOR

BORIS LEONIDOVICH PASTERNAK, both winner and rejector of the Nobel Prize for Literature for 1958, poet, novelist, and outstandingly gifted translator of Goethe and Shakespeare, was born in Moscow in 1890 and died in disgrace at his home in the so-called "writer's village" of Peredelkino in May, 1960.

Although best known in the West for his monumental novel *Doctor Zhivago,* the cause of his political downfall, he is most highly regarded in his native country as a poet.

Of all his poetry, it is *Sister My Life,* written in 1917 and first published in 1922, that has always remained the most popular and is considered by the majority of critics to be the finest of his lyrical works.

ABOUT THE TRANSLATOR

PHILLIP C. FLAYDERMAN, teacher, poet, and translator, is Editorial Director of Walker Educational Book Company. He gives courses at the School of Continuing Education of New York University in the Fundamentals of Editing and in the Great Tradition of Russian Literature — Pushkin to Pasternak.